THE
STRENGTH
CODE

A Practical Blueprint for Building Unshakable
Strength in Christ and Taking Back What's Yours

LARRY & DENISE ADEBESIN

Copyright © 2025 by Larry and Denise Adebesin

All rights reserved.

No part of this book may be reproduced, stored in a retrieval system,or transmitted in any form or by any means—electronic, mechanical,photocopying, recording, or otherwise—without the prior written permission of the publisher, except in the case of brief quotations embodied in critical articles or reviews.

TABLE OF CONTENTS

Introduction	1
Chapter 1: Unlocking the Benefits of Salvation	11
Chapter 2: The Battle You're In	21
Chapter 3: It Is Finished	31
Chapter 4: Your Identity in Christ	49
Chapter 5: Building Spiritual Strength	57
Chapter 6: Power of Angels	65
Chapter 7: The Power of the Blood	71
Chapter 8: The Power of the Holy Spirit	91
Chapter 9: Power in Jesus's Name	101
Chapter 10: Power of the Word	113
Chapter 11: Activating Your Spiritual Weapons	121
Chapter 12: Using Your Weapons	127
Chapter 13: Power of Faith	131
Chapter 14: Growing Your Faith	137
Chapter 15: Faith Through Delays	155
Chapter 16: Never Lose a Battle Again	163
Acknowledgement	177
About the Authors	178

INTRODUCTION

THE TRANSFORMATIVE POWER OF BIBLICAL PRINCIPLES

Within the pages of this spiritual guide lies the key to unlocking profound personal transformation through the consistent application of biblical principles. Believers who embrace these teachings can expect a cascade of blessings—ranging from unshakeable faith to victorious living. The principles outlined not only reinforce spiritual resilience but also ensure a life aligned with divine purpose.

Consider Hannah, a struggling single mother overwhelmed by life's burdens and on the brink of despair. Upon integrating these principles—steadfast prayer, rigorous study of God's Word, and active participation in her faith community—Hannah experienced a remarkable turnaround. Her faith blossomed from mere mustard seed size to the mountain-moving kind that Jesus spoke of in Mark 11:23. This empowerment translated into practical victories: she resolved financial struggles miraculously, witnessed her family's healing, and found peace in areas previously marked by turmoil.

By embracing a lifestyle built on spiritual discipline and unwavering faith, like Hannah, individuals can harness the boundless power of God's promises. This book offers a roadmap not just for momentary relief but for enduring transformation in spirit, mind, and body. It demonstrates how aligning our daily lives with divine principles leads to unparalleled strength and peace, ushering believers into a life of continuous victory and fulfillment. Through real-life stories and actionable insights, each chapter serves as a step closer to not just imagining but living a life of faith-fueled triumph.

Who This Book Is For

This book is for people who believe in the promises of the Bible, who have tried to experience them but have not been successful so far. It is not for those who want something for nothing. You are not required to do anything in this guide to make it to heaven, except receive Jesus as your Lord and Savior. However, to enjoy heavenly benefits such as love, joy, peace, power, abundance, good health, and positive relationships on earth, there are requirements.

This guide is designed to help you evaluate your results. If you like the results you are getting, more power to you; we bless the Lord for you. If you don't like your results and would like to find out what might be wrong or out of place and what you must do to fix them, you're in the right place. This is a guide for those who are willing to accept and take individual responsibility.

A Note from the Authors

The information contained in this book is based on our understanding of the scriptures and our experiences studying the Word and attending many workshops, conferences, and seminars for over 30 years. Please take what you find helpful and adjust it as the Holy Spirit leads you.

Definition of The Strength Code

The Strength Code is a spiritual framework aimed at empowering believers to build unshakable strength in Christ. It offers a blueprint for reclaiming personal victories by leveraging specific divine tools and principles. The core idea revolves around using spiritual weapons—Angels, the Blood, the Holy Spirit, the Name of Jesus, and the Word of God—to strengthen one's faith and overcome life's challenges. Each component contributes uniquely to the overall strength and resilience of a believer, fostering a life of victory and alignment with divine purpose.

The Strength Code Formula

The Strength Code = (Angels + Blood + Holy Spirit + Name of Jesus + Word)

- **Angels**: Serve as messengers and protectors, responding to God's commands and aiding believers in spiritual warfare.

- **Blood (of Jesus)**: Acts as a redeeming and protective shield, symbolizing victory over sin and adversities.

- **Holy Spirit**: Empowers, guides, and intercedes, providing believers with the strength and wisdom necessary for spiritual growth.

- **Name of Jesus**: Holds ultimate authority, offering protection and breakthrough in every realm of life.

- **Word of God**: The foundation of faith, delivering clarity, healing, and guidance, acting as a sword in spiritual battles.

By integrating these elements, believers can effectively engage in spiritual warfare and achieve unmovable strength in Christ.

How to Get the Most from This Book

This book is designed to take you from where you are to where you want to be—from small strength to great strength in every area of your life, whether it be physically, mentally, emotionally, financially, or spiritually. The following suggestions will help you do just that:

1. **Plan to Get Stronger**

   Set aside a definite time daily to think, plan, study, and grow in all areas of your life. Do not pray for your problems to become easier; instead, pray and plan to become stronger.

2. **Decide What You Want**

   Before you start reading this book, identify at least one area in each of the above categories where you would like to get stronger. This will help you recognize the principles and ideas that will be most useful in reaching those objectives.

3. **Personalize the Book**

   Imagine that the authors are speaking to you alone. Make the content resonate with your personal journey.

4. **Study the Book**

   Do more than just read; study the book. Read it repeatedly with a pen and highlighter, underlining the areas that apply to you the most.

5. **Apply the Principles**

   Address your situation by recognizing, relating to, and assimilating the principles. Allow these principles to become part of you and expect them to evolve from you.

6. **Memorize Key Phrases**

   Memorize quotations and key phrases that are meaningful to you. This will help you internalize these principles and practice the art of biblical meditation to some degree.

7. **Listen to the Audio Version**

   Listening to the audio version of this book can help you engage different parts of your brain and retain information more effectively.

8. **Share These Principles**

   Conduct and lead a study group to share these principles with others. This is a great opportunity to put the strength code formula into action. Go for it and grow stronger.

How to Get the Most from the Strength Code

To fully harness the benefits of "The Strength Code," approach this guide with an open heart and a willingness to engage deeply with its principles. Begin by familiarizing yourself with the core concepts introduced in the initial chapters, which lay the foundation for understanding spiritual warfare. These chapters detail the key tools and strategies that will be your arsenal for developing strength and resilience in your spiritual journey.

Integrate the practical exercises and action plans outlined in each chapter into your daily routine. These include practices such as daily devotions, implementing the full armor of God, regular prayer, and actively using the spiritual weapons highlighted in the book. By consistently applying these techniques, you cultivate a disciplined spiritual life that fosters growth and transformation.

Embrace the stories and testimonies shared throughout the book as sources of inspiration and evidence of the principles in action. Let these narratives reinforce your faith and motivate you to seek similar breakthroughs in your personal spiritual journey.

Finally, commit to continual reflection and adaptation of the teachings to suit your life circumstances. Engage with the end-of-chapter call-to-action segments to evaluate your progress and explore new ways to challenge yourself. By actively living out the principles and maintaining a journal of your experiences, you will enhance the depth and effectiveness of your engagement with "The Strength Code," ensuring enduring spiritual resilience and empowerment.

What "The Strength Code" Will Do for You

"The Strength Code" offers readers a comprehensive framework to transform their spiritual lives by building unshakable strength in Christ. Here are ten key takeaways from this insightful guide:

- **Transition from Weak Faith to Great Faith**: Learn how to grow your faith from a fragile state into one that is powerful and resilient.

- **Harness Spiritual Weapons**: Understand the significance and application of spiritual tools like the blood of Jesus, the Holy Spirit, and the Word.

- **Identity in Christ**: Discover your true identity as a believer, including being loved, forgiven, and empowered.

- **Develop Spiritual Resilience**: Build spiritual muscle through disciplined daily practices that fortify your faith.

- **Engage in Effective Spiritual Warfare**: Master strategies for defending against spiritual attacks and standing firm in victory.

- **Understand the Power of the Holy Spirit**: Explore how the Holy Spirit empowers and guides you into all truth.

- **Apply the Power of the Blood**: Utilize the blood of Jesus to declare victory over every adversarial circumstance.

- **Grow Through Trials**: Embrace spiritual delays as opportunities for growth and increased trust in God's timing.

- **Overcome Life's Challenges**: Discover practical steps for applying faith to overcome financial, health, and relational obstacles.

- **Prepare for Continuous Victory**: Sustain your spiritual growth and ensure lasting change by implementing a personalized action plan.

CHAPTER 1

UNLOCKING THE BENEFITS OF SALVATION

What is Spiritual Warfare?

"This guide is all about spiritual warfare—the invisible battle between the Kingdom of God and the forces of darkness. This isn't a fight with fists or weapons, but a battle fought in the spiritual realm. Many believers struggle to enjoy the full benefits of their salvation not because God is withholding anything, but because they're unaware of this spiritual conflict. Without recognizing the battle and applying intentional, biblical strategies, it's easy to live beneath your inheritance. This chapter will help you uncover the true nature of this battle and show you how to walk in the victory Christ has already secured for you.

Identifying the Battlefield

The battlefield of spiritual warfare includes:

- **The Mind** – The enemy plants lies, doubts, and fears to weaken your faith (2 Corinthians 10:5).
- **Your Faith** – The enemy seeks to shake your trust in God's promises (1 Timothy 6:12).
- **Your Authority** – If you do not know who you are in Christ, you cannot walk in victory (Luke 10:19).
- **Your Destiny** – The enemy tries to hinder God's plans for your life (Jeremiah 29:11).

Now that you understand where the enemy often strikes, it's time to evaluate how prepared you are to stand your ground. Just as a soldier regularly trains for battle, a believer must develop spiritual habits that build endurance and power. The following self-assessment will help you identify which spiritual disciplines are thriving in your life—and which ones need attention.

What Is Your Level of Discipleship (Discipline)

Before you take the quiz below, please remember this is not to condemn you; there is no condemnation for you because you are in Christ Jesus. The purpose of this quiz is to help evaluate how closely you have followed some of the main biblical principles that lead to success in the Kingdom. While some believers may walk in blessings without fully practicing these disciplines, intentionally embracing them empowers you to walk in greater authority, clarity, and spiritual breakthrough.

The important thing to know is that if you score zero on the quiz, this guide will help you reach the top speedily if you prayerfully apply the principles with the help of the Holy Spirit. Denise and I are rooting for you and are here to assist you in any way we can. We pray for everyone who will ever be exposed to this guide to have a Divine Encounter that will catapult you to greatness and numerous breakthroughs, in the Name of Jesus.

Willingness and Obedience Questionnaire

Here's a simplified list of spiritual disciplines designed to cultivate faith and resilience in spiritual warfare. Reflect on each one to assess your current practice levels:

- **Putting on the Full Armor of God Daily**: Imagine starting each day by visualizing putting on the armor. For Linda, before stepping out of bed, she mentally 'puts on' the belt of truth, the breastplate of righteousness, and the other pieces, much like she would dress for work, reminding herself that she is protected against life's challenges because of her faith (Ephesians 6:10-18).

- **Regular Weekly Church Attendance**: For Scott, attending church isn't just an obligation. Every Sunday, he anticipates joyfully meeting with his church family, encouraged by their collective sharing and learning. He aims to attend at least 42 weeks a year, reserving Sundays as a non-negotiable time for spiritual renewal and community connection (Hebrews 10:24-25).

- **Regular Weekly Fasting**: Maria incorporates fasting into her week by skipping two meals on Wednesdays. With medical clearance, she uses this time for personal reflection and prayer, focusing on aligning her life with her spiritual goals. (Luke 18:12)

- **Consistent Giving**: John sets aside 10% of his income every payday, viewing it as a physical commitment to prioritize God in his finances. Over time, he has experienced blessings such as unexpected savings and peace regarding his financial decisions. (Malachi 3:10-12)

- **Daily Prayer Habit**: Set aside a consistent time each morning—perhaps while your coffee brews—to speak with God. This could be a simple prayer of gratitude, a plea for strength, or praying through a list of loved ones. (Luke 18:1)

- **Habit of Giving Thanks Regularly**: Tom writes down three things he's thankful for each night, whether they are mundane or significant. This practice fosters a sense of fulfillment and appreciation for daily blessings. (1 Thessalonians 5:18)

- **Rejoicing Evermore**: During her daily commute, Emily listens to worship music, choosing joy even in the face of traffic frustrations. Rejoicing becomes a voluntary act and a reminder of greater truths beyond her current circumstances. (1 Thessalonians 5:17)

- **Daily Bible Reading and Meditation**: Alex spends ten to thirty minutes each morning in quiet reflection, reading a few chapters and pondering their application to his day. This practice helps him feel connected to a larger purpose and narrative. (Joshua 1:8)

- **Serving the Lord with Gladness**: Lisa engages regularly each week by volunteering at a local shelter. She finds purpose in serving others, and her meaningful interactions bring joy and gratitude to both her and those she assists. (Psalm 100:2)

- **Daily Confession and Declaration of God's Word**: Each day, David speaks affirmations aloud, declaring scriptures that align with his values and goals. Starting with a whisper, this practice builds his faith and confidence in God's promises. (Luke 21:15)

Evaluating Your Faith's Development:

- Your score doesn't measure your worth; it highlights your spiritual readiness for the battles you face. Assign a score of 10 to any discipline you practice regularly for at least four days a week.

- A score above 80 indicates that you're strengthening your defenses. Scores between 60 and 80 suggest your foundation is solid but in need of reinforcement. A score below 60 is not a defeat; it signals a need to re-arm and rebuild. Use the following steps to begin that recovery process today.

- Greater than 80: Indicates Growth/Strength
- 70-80: You're Playing it Safe
- 60-70: Risky Territory
- Under 60: Risky with Potential Frustrations

Steps to Spiritual Recovery and Victory:

Embarking on a journey of spiritual recovery involves transforming habits and reclaiming the victorious life that Christ has promised. By intentionally breaking negative patterns and forming new, life-giving ones, you can develop robust spiritual disciplines. Here's a guide merged with practical steps to assist you on this path:

Break Your Current Pattern

Purpose: Identify and disrupt behaviors that hinder spiritual growth.

- Recognize habitual actions or mindsets that need to change.
- Reflect on how these patterns impact your spiritual health.

- Decide to remove or replace one habit at a time, focusing on positive change.

Form a New Pattern and Infuse It with Life

Purpose: Establish and nurture healthier spiritual habits.

- Choose practices that align with your spiritual goals and begin integrating them into your daily life.
- Infuse each new habit with intention, ensuring it's not just routine but a life-enhancing experience.
- Commit to patience and persistence, understanding that growth takes time.

Next Steps Action Plan for Developing Spiritual Discipline

Purpose: Provide actionable measures to strengthen your spiritual foundation.

- **Commit to Daily Spiritual Habits:**
    - Read the Bible and meditate for 30 minutes daily. If needed, divide this into two 15-minute sessions—morning and evening—to ensure consistency.
- **Gradual Increase in Church Attendance:**
    - If attendance has been sporadic, commit to one weekly service. Join a

small group for support, gradually increasing your attendance to 42 or more weeks per year.

- **Incorporate Fasting and Generosity:**
  - Begin by fasting one meal weekly, keeping health precautions in mind. Align your giving to 10% of your income, practicing discipline and faithfulness.

- **Develop a Strong Prayer Routine:**
  - Start daily prayers with a 10-minute goal, gradually extending as you become more comfortable. Use prompts or scriptures to enrich your focus and consistency.

- **Cultivate a Spirit of Gratitude and Joy:**
  - Express gratitude throughout your day to transform your mindset and increase resilience. Endeavor to find joy in all circumstances, shifting your perspective positively.

Monitoring Your Progress

Purpose: Track and refine your journey for continued growth.

- **Track Your Habits:** Use a journal or digital app to log and mark daily disciplines as you build consistency.

- **Evaluate Monthly:** Reflect each month on your progress, noting areas for improvement, adjusting goals, and celebrating achievements.

Action Plan Recap

- **Understand the Battlefield**: Recognize that spiritual warfare involves battling against lies and doubts planted in your mind, attacks on your faith, challenges to your authority, and threats to your destiny. Equip yourself with knowledge from the Scriptures (Ephesians 6:12-13, 2 Corinthians 10:3-5) and affirm your identity in Christ.

- **Adopt Strategic Practices**: Engage in daily spiritual disciplines such as putting on the full armor of God, regular church attendance, fasting as guided by health considerations, consistent giving, daily prayer, and scripture engagement. These practices form the foundation of your spiritual strategy.

- **Evaluate and Develop Your Faith**: Regularly assess the development of your faith with a reflective quiz to identify areas for spiritual growth. Scores above 80 indicate strong growth, while lower scores suggest areas needing attention.

- **Break and Reshape Habits**: Identify and break unproductive patterns in your spiritual life while forming new, life-affirming habits that align with God's will. This deliberate effort helps ensure recovery and continuous victory in spiritual battles.

- **Seek Continuous Improvement**: Remember that improvement in spiritual warfare involves acknowledging shortcomings, applying core biblical principles, and embracing the guidance of the Holy Spirit to achieve spiritual breakthroughs.

CHAPTER 2

THE BATTLE YOU'RE IN

Understanding the Nature of the Battle

"To fully recover what belongs to us—and ensure we never lose another battle—we must first understand the nature of the battle we're fighting."

Ephesians 6:10-19 summarizes the nature of the battle and how to win it. Revelation Chapter 12 reveals that the real battle is between God and the devil. The devil was cast out of heaven and is now angry at God's children, you and me, who live on earth. Revelation 12:8 states that the dragon did not prevail. This means that as long as we call upon Angelic Reinforcement—invoking God's angels through prayer and scriptural authority—the devil and his agents will never prevail against us.

This is a spiritual battle, not a physical one.

Refer to 2 Corinthians 10:3-5 and Ephesians 6:10-13 for further insight. In Ephesians 6:10-13, we learn that we wrestle against principalities and powers.

To bring this spiritual reality closer to home, let's examine the journey of one believer who discovered these truths in his own life. In a peaceful small town, Alex, a devoted family man, was living a seemingly conflict-free life until a series of unexplained setbacks disrupted his tranquility. Despite his faith, Alex felt overwhelmed and ill-equipped to handle the mounting pressures. Bills piled up, health concerns arose, and relationships strained. Little did he realize that his struggles were more than mere chance; he was entrenched in a spiritual battleground.

Initially unaware of the spiritual dimensions behind his challenges, Alex faced obstacles with limited success, blaming external circumstances. His turning point came during a church service when Ephesians 6:10-18 was read, highlighting the unseen forces at play and the spiritual armor necessary for victory. As the words washed over him, Alex felt an awakening inside. For the first time, he understood that his struggles weren't random—they had a spiritual root. He realized he hadn't been fighting back spiritually, and tears welled up as he made a decision to change course. Inspired, Alex delved into biblical teachings on spiritual warfare, understanding for the first time the significance of his trials.

Empowered by this revelation, Alex began integrating disciplined prayer and scriptural declarations into his daily routine, equipping himself with God's armor. He embraced the authority of Jesus' name and learned to reinforce his faith through consistent engagement with the Word. Gradually, Alex noticed changes. His finances stabilized, health improved, and relationships healed. What seemed impossible before now became achievable—mountains were moved not by force, but by faith.

As Alex continued on this path, sharing his journey with others, he realized that the key to overcoming lay not only in understanding the nature of his battles but also in the consistent application of spiritual principles. His transformation not only changed his life but also inspired his community, demonstrating that any believer, with the right tools and understanding, can turn adversity into triumph. Through Alex's story, the profound impact of recognizing and engaging in spiritual warfare stands as a testament to the power and victory found in a life anchored in faith.

Colossians 2:13-15 tells us that these principalities have already been disarmed.

Ephesians 1:19-2:6 tells us they are under our feet.

If Jesus has already defeated those who oppose us, all we need to do is engage the opposition, challenges, issues, and concerns confronting us in the Name or Authority of Jesus, and we too will defeat them every time. That's why Ephesians 6:10-19 instructs us to put on the whole armor of God, so we can render every activity and operation of the enemy null, void, and ineffective.

The armor of God is our uniform, our ID card showing we are in Christ; hence we are invincible as long as we take our place and stand our ground.

Your Problem Is *NOT* The Real Problem

With this background in mind, let us look at Proverbs 24:10. According to Proverbs 24:10, if we falter in times of trouble, our strength is small, indicating that our problem is not the problem. This reveals that our biggest challenge isn't the trouble itself, but the strength we bring to face it. "O ye of little faith," you have faith, you have strength, but it's not enough to confront and overcome the opposition (Matthew 8:26). Jesus told the disciples they had little faith or strength because they were supposed to have great faith by now due to their position in Christ, but their experience showed otherwise.

This is why spiritual strength training is essential—so we never again fall short when adversity strikes. That stops now. By the time you finish going through this Guide, you will have your very own 7-day, 30-day, 90-day, and 1-year plan to start with.

Introduction to Spiritual Strength Training

To win every spiritual battle, we need more than momentary inspiration—we need ongoing strength. Just as athletes train daily to stay in peak condition, believers must spiritually train to remain victorious. Engaging in spiritual warfare requires more than just passive faith; it demands a dynamic and consistent approach to strengthening one's spiritual muscles. This concept of **spiritual strength training** parallels physical exercise routines and ensures that believers are equipped to face life's challenges with resilience and power. Here's how structured spiritual practices, akin to gym exercises, can influence various aspects of life:

1. **Warm-Up: Daily Devotion (Stretching)**
   - *Spiritual Benefit*: Prepares the mind and spirit for the day's challenges.
   - *Life Impact*: Sets a tone of focus and peace, enhancing clarity in financial decisions and relationship interactions.

2. **Cardio: Prayer and Fasting (Aerobic Exercise)**
   - *Spiritual Benefit*: Builds endurance and patience.
   - *Life Impact*: Supports perseverance through financial or marital struggles, fostering patience and long-term vision.

3. **Strength Training: Putting on the Full Armor of God (Resistance Workouts)**
   - *Spiritual Benefit*: Fortifies against spiritual and emotional challenges.
   - *Life Impact*: Enhances resilience in health battles, promoting a strong mindset against adversity.

4. **Flexibility: Practicing Forgiveness and Gratitude (Dynamic Stretching)**
   - *Spiritual Benefit*: Promotes mental and emotional flexibility.

- *Life Impact*: Eases tensions in marriage and personal relationships, fostering a harmonious environment.

5. **Core Strength: Bible Study and Meditation (Core Workouts)**
    - *Spiritual Benefit*: Solidifies core beliefs and values.
    - *Life Impact*: Provides a stable foundation for ethical financial decisions, harmonious relationships, and a health-conscious lifestyle.

The following table illustrates how each spiritual discipline affects key areas of life. As you reflect on these connections, consider where you need the most growth and how your spiritual routine can support that transformation.

Table: The Impact of Spiritual Strength on Life Areas

Spiritual Exercise	Financial Impact	Marital Impact	Health Impact
Daily Devotion	Enhances decision-making clarity	Promotes peace and understanding	Boosts mental clarity for better health choices
Prayer and Fasting	Encourages patience and strategic investments	Fosters deepened emotional connection	Supports detoxification and mental resilience

Full Armor of God	Builds confidence in risk-taking (within ethical limits)	Strengthens conflict resolution skills	Enhances immune response through mental strength
Forgiveness and Gratitude	Eases the burden of financial stress	Cultivates harmonious relationship dynamics	Promotes overall well-being and reduces stress
Bible Study and Meditation	Grounded principles guide spending and saving tactics	Establishes a foundation of shared values	Encourages healthier lifestyle choices

By mapping these spiritual disciplines onto areas of life such as finances, marriage, and health, believers can systematically develop their spiritual strength. This holistic approach ensures they are prepared for spiritual warfare and equipped to transform adversity into victory across all facets of life.

Make these declarations:

First Declaration: "In the Name of Jesus, I forget the past and all the errors and mistakes of the past. I reach forth to those things which are before, which Christ obtained for me and apprehended me for. I Go Forward!" (Romans 8:1-2, Philippians 3:12-14)

Second Declaration: "I am a new creation in Christ. I press forward by grace and with determination to possess my possessions." (2 Peter 1:3-4, Numbers 13:30, Matthew 9:29)

Action Plan Recap

1. **Embrace Spiritual Strength Training:**

- Recognize the necessity of intentionally building spiritual resilience, much like physical exercise. Establish a routine analogous to a gym regimen, incorporating daily devotion (stretching), prayer and fasting (cardio), and Bible study (core workouts).

- This regimen strengthens faith like muscles, preparing you for life's spiritual battles.

2. **Equip Yourself with the Full Armor of God:**

- Follow the biblical directive in Ephesians 6:10-18 to wear the full armor of God daily. This is your spiritual "uniform," providing protection and identity as a believer, enabling you to stand firm against spiritual opposition.

3. **Transform Weakness into Strength:**

- Identify areas of weakness exposed in spiritual battles. By applying the principles from this guide, create a personalized spiritual strength plan (7 days, 30 days, 90 days, and 1 year) that targets areas needing development. This plan will incrementally build stamina and faith.

4. Implement Forgiveness and Gratitude Practices:

- Cultivate flexibility in faith through regular practices of forgiveness and gratitude. This warms the heart and mind, alleviates stress, and enhances relational harmony, thereby improving overall well-being and readiness for spiritual battles.

5. Apply Biblical Declarations in Everyday Life:

- Use powerful declarations to reinforce spiritual truths and identity, such as reclaiming your new creation status in Christ and setting your sights on divine promises. Consistent use of these declarations transforms thoughts and strengthens resolve.

By systematically implementing these actions, you not only prepare for spiritual warfare but also position yourself for success in various life areas, embodying God's promises through everyday application.

CHAPTER 3

IT IS FINISHED

John 19:30 tells us, "It is finished." This means every challenge—physical, mental, financial, emotional, relational, spiritual, or even demonic—has already been defeated by Jesus. Whether your struggle lies in health, career, legal matters, or inner turmoil, know this: Jesus has already handled it. Our role now is to learn how to rest in His victory by learning of Him (Matthew 11:28–30; 1 Corinthians 15:57–58).

The theological message underlying "It is finished" in John 19:30 is enriched by several other biblical passages, each adding layers to our understanding of salvation, freedom, and prophecy fulfillment.

Hebrews 10:10-14 elaborates on the concept of Jesus as the *once-for-all sacrifice*, emphasizing that His death eradicated the repetitive need for sacrifices previously required under the law. This single, ultimate sacrifice underscores the completeness and sufficiency of Christ's atoning work, offering believers assurance that their redemption is irrevocably secured.

Romans 8:1-2 introduces the theme of *freedom in Christ*, pronouncing that there is no condemnation for those who are in Christ Jesus. Through His sacrifice, believers are liberated from the law of sin and death, cementing our victory and freedom through His resurrection power.

Isaiah 53:5, a prophetic foretelling of Jesus' suffering, declares that *by His wounds, we are healed*. This passage highlights the fulfillment of prophecy and confirms the redemptive purpose of Jesus' sacrifice, which is meant to restore and heal, providing a foundational promise accessible to believers.

Together, these passages assure that through Christ's finished work, believers can live in a state of freedom and victory over all aspects of sin and adversity. This interconnected understanding encourages a life of faith and rest in Jesus' completed work, inviting believers to embrace this truth fully.

After committing to the understanding of the finished work of Christ exemplified in John 19:30, along with insights from Hebrews 10:10-14, Romans 8:1-2, and Isaiah 53:5, consider the transformative story of Mark, a businessman who struggled with anxiety and self-doubt. He wrestled with sleepless nights, continually plagued by thoughts of inadequacy and past failures.

One day, during a particularly low period, Mark participated in a small group study focusing on the *finality* of Christ's sacrifice. The group delved into Hebrews, emphasizing the *once-for-all* nature of Jesus' atonement, illuminating how it offered both forgiveness and *freedom* from self-condemnation, as noted in Romans. Mark realized he was not living in this truth; his perception was still trapped in striving and fear.

As he began to integrate this knowledge, grounding his faith in the prophetic promise of *healing* found in Isaiah, he experienced a profound shift. His prayers transformed from desperate pleas to quiet, confident declarations of the victory already won for him through Christ. Over the weeks, Mark's anxiety diminished as he embraced this liberating truth, allowing him to rest in Jesus' completed work. Encouraged by Romans 8:1-2, he accepted that there was truly no condemnation for him, significantly impacting his personal and professional life, freeing him to focus on opportunities, not failures.

This story encapsulates the life-changing potential available when individuals fully grasp and embrace the implications of Christ's finished work. It serves as a testament to the *wholeness* and *peace* promised to believers when we rest in the truth of Christ's comprehensive victory over life's challenges.

Practical Reflection Exercise

As you reflect on the message of "It is finished," consider this simple yet powerful exercise to help ground your faith and find peace in Christ's victory over your struggles:

1. **List Your Top Three Struggles:** Take a moment to identify and write down the three significant challenges you're currently facing in your life, whether they are physical, emotional, financial, or spiritual.

2. **Declare Victory:** Next to each listed struggle, write the words "It is Finished." This act symbolically acknowledges that the power and resolution of these issues have been completed by Jesus' sacrifice and victory.

3. **Offer Thanksgiving:** After writing "It is Finished" beside each struggle, express your gratitude by writing a brief note of thanksgiving. Thank Jesus for His ultimate sacrifice and the freedom it grants over these burdens.

This exercise serves as a reminder to shift your focus from the burden of problem-solving on your own to resting in the assured triumph found in faith. Engaging in this practice regularly can reinforce a mindset of peace and trust, encouraging you to lean more into spiritual truths and find comfort in His promises.

Devotional: Embracing "It is Finished"

In the final moments on the cross, Jesus declared, "It is finished" (John 19:30), a profound statement that redefines a believer's relationship with their past, present, and future. These words encapsulate the completion of His mission to redeem humanity, offering undeniable assurance of victory over sin and death.

For past failures, this declaration invites believers to cast aside lingering guilt and shame. The power of past mistakes is nullified by Christ's ultimate sacrifice, emphasizing that redemption is not contingent on one's merits but on His finished work. This liberation allows believers to move forward unencumbered, embracing the fresh start offered by God's grace.

Current struggles take on a new dimension under the shadow of the cross. Challenges, whether they manifest as emotional, financial, or spiritual, are absorbed into the triumph of Christ's pronouncement. His victory alleviates the burden of fighting battles alone, inviting believers to rest in His sufficiency. In every valley, they can find solace knowing that Jesus has navigated and overcome every trial.

Looking ahead, "It is finished" transforms future hopes from aspiring dreams to assured realities. This assurance empowers believers to look forward with confident expectation. Scripture promises that God's plans are to prosper, not to harm, and to bring a hopeful future (Jeremiah 29:11). With Christ's declaration, the uncertainty of what is to come is overshadowed by the certainty of His enduring victory.

By embracing "It is finished," believers are called to live lives marked by bold faith and assured hope, standing confidently in the victory already won. As we align our lives with this truth, we become living testaments of His unending grace and completed work.

Thank You Jesus

As you cultivate gratitude, remember that your thanksgiving is not in vain—it's rooted in the victory Jesus has already secured. Let's look deeper into what that victory means in the spiritual realm. Your problems, issues, or situations are completely and totally solved; it was already so over 2000 years ago. That's why "**Thank You Jesus**" is one of the most effective and faith-filled prayers you can pray. Do it right now. Say "**Thank You Jesus**" 10 times, 20 times, 50 times, etc., and mean it. Make it a habit to do this every hour you are awake, and watch your life change for the better. A grateful heart attracts more blessings (1 Thessalonians 5:18, Ephesians 5:20, Psalm 92:1-2). What are you saying Thank You Jesus for? Everything that is working in your life and everything that you think is not perfect yet, because Jesus took care of it all; you just are not aware of it yet. Philemon 1:6 says whatever we acknowledge becomes more effective in our lives.

The Power of Repetitive Praise: A Journey of Transformation

The simple practice of saying "Thank You, Jesus" every hour can profoundly reshape your spiritual and emotional state. Beyond a mere act of gratitude, this repetitive praise engages both mind and spirit, fostering significant personal transformation—akin to the process described in Romans 12:2 as the "renewing of your mind."

Neuroscience and Gratitude

Scientific research in neuroscience shows that gratitude can reshape our brain's neural pathways. When you repeatedly express gratitude, the brain's neurochemicals like dopamine and serotonin are activated, enhancing mood and emotional regulation. This practice aligns beautifully with the biblical principle of renewing our minds, emphasizing a transformational process through consistent, positive affirmations.

Tracking Your Transformation

To truly grasp the impact of this practice, consider tracking your spiritual and emotional changes over a set period—7, 14, or 30 days. By monitoring your mood, attitude, and outlook daily, you gain concrete insights into how this practice influences your life. Note changes in stress levels, emotional responses, and overall happiness.

Journaling Your Journey

To document your breakthroughs, use a simple journaling template:

1. **Grateful Acknowledgement:** "Today, I say 'Thank You, Jesus' for..."
2. **Daily Reflection:** "I noticed today that..."
3. **Transformation Note:** "One area I feel a shift in is..."
4. **Future Hopes:** "I'm hopeful that..."

Embrace these reflections as a testament to your spiritual journey, serving as a mirror of transformation over time.

Practical Application

Begin today by setting an hourly reminder. When it chimes, pause to say, "Thank You, Jesus," focusing wholeheartedly on its significance. As you practice this regularly, in line with (Psalm 92:1-2 and Ephesians 5:20), you're likely to observe a noticeable shift in your spiritual and emotional dimensions. Each moment of gratitude rewrites your emotional script—inviting peace, anchoring faith, and ultimately transforming how you perceive daily challenges and future possibilities.

This exercise in gratitude and praise not only uplifts your spirit but also strengthens your mental fortitude. As you engage consistently in this practice, you will witness a gradual yet powerful transformation in your life, grounded in faith and the Psalmist's assurance of God's unceasing faithfulness.

Jesus Has Already Disarmed ALL Your Enemies

Colossians 2:13-15 states that all powers responsible for your challenges have been disarmed, destroyed, nullified, and vanquished in the spiritual realm. They know this, and they also know you may not be aware yet, which is why they continue to harass you (1 Peter 5:8). Their time is up right now. It's time for you to enforce your victory (1 Corinthians 15:57-58, 2 Corinthians 2:14).

Pray like this:

Father, by the blood of Jesus, I decree the complete and total destruction of any power resisting me in any area of my life, in the Name of Jesus.

How to Use This Prayer:

- *Speak it out loud to build faith (Romans 10:17)*
- *Be specific about the area you are praying for—health, finances, relationships*
- *Repeat it daily as part of your spiritual routine*
- *Visualize your rightful place as a victorious child of God.*

Faith comes by hearing (Romans 10:17), so when you pray the Word out loud, you hear it, and faith is released through speaking (Matthew 17:20, Luke 17:6, 2 Corinthians 4:13). We overcome by faith (1

John 5:4). When you open your mouth (Psalm 81:10-14) and speak, you release fire that can consume all your opposition (James 3:6, Hebrews 12:19, Jeremiah 23:29). By praying out loud, you resist the opposition while building your faith. You are increasing your strength, which is essential to stand in the day of trouble (Proverbs 24:10). When you pray according to the Word of God, you inflict pain on the enemy because angels carry out the sayings of the Word (Psalm 103:20, Revelation 22:9, Daniel 10:13-14), and the dragon cannot prevail against them (Revelation 12:8, Revelation 12:11, Daniel 10:13-14).

Galatians 3:13-14 declares that we have been fully redeemed.

The Problem and the **Only** Solution!!!

The real problem is our weakness and lack of knowledge of who we are in Christ and what Jesus has already accomplished for us.

Three-Tiered Model of Spiritual Warfare

In our journey through spiritual warfare, adopting a strategic approach can foster resilience, faith, and victory. Here's a three-tiered model to navigate these challenges: Recognize the Lie, Speak the Truth, and Declare Victory.

1. Recognize the Lie

Identifying deception is the first step in combating spiritual adversity. As referenced in Colossians 2:13-15, the powers against us have been disarmed; however, they persist in deluding us into feeling powerless. The enemy thrives on misinformation, exploiting our lack of awareness about our spiritual authority in Christ. Awareness and discernment are crucial to unveil these lies. Remember, 1 Peter 5:8 warns of the enemy's prowling nature, underscoring the importance of vigilance.

2. Speak the Truth

Once the lie is unveiled, counter it with truth. This principle is exemplified from the beginning in Genesis 1, where God employs speech to manifest reality. Similarly, Jesus countered demonic forces with direct verbal commands. Speaking truth aloud enforces its potency, rooted in Romans 10:17 and Matthew 17:20, emphasizing faith through auditory reinforcement. When you decree, as shown in scriptural instances like Hebrews 4:12, you wield the Word's sword to dismantle lies and affirm God's promises over your life.

3. Declare Victory

Finally, boldly declare the victory won through Christ, affirming the defeat of spiritual adversaries. This is not merely a reclamation of what is but an enforcement of what has already been wrought. Practice prayers such as: "Father, by the blood of Jesus, I decree the complete destruction of any power resisting me," as an audible assertion of triumph. Through this, as suggested in 1 Corinthians 15:57-58, believers stand firm in victory, assured that their challenges are nullified.

Practical Applications and Case Studies

Throughout history and in personal testimonies, we see believers fortified through the three-tier methodology. Take Anna, a woman who overcame chronic anxiety by vocalizing truths and declaring victory through scripture-based prayers. Her testimony illuminates the transition from fear to peace, showcasing the effectiveness of the model.

Wrap-Up

By engaging in this model, you not only resist opposition but nurture fertile ground for spiritual and emotional renewal, aligning with Proverbs 24:10 for strength in adversity. This approach empowers you to live as a testament to Christ's victory over darkness, instilling a spirit of unwavering faith and assurance.

Spiritual Strength in Crisis Times

Understanding Crisis: The Nature of Unexpected Turmoil

A *crisis* is an unanticipated event that disrupts life, challenging our emotional, spiritual, and physical reserves. It tests resolve and faith, often arriving when least expected. From sudden loss to global disasters, crises force us to confront uncertainties and fears, demanding spiritual resilience and readiness to face the unpredictable.

Now that we've established the spiritual truth that your victory is already won in Christ, let's explore how to live that out practically—especially in times of crisis. The next sections will equip you with spiritual tools and habits to navigate tough moments with strength and peace.

Developing a Crisis Response Plan

Immediate Reactions: In moments of crisis, it's essential to ground yourself in faith. Recognize the initial emotional wave and create a space for immediate prayer, anchoring your spirit. *Philippians 4:6-7* counsels, "Do not be anxious about anything, but in every situation, by prayer and petition, with thanksgiving, present your requests to God."

Building a Network: Establish a support system composed of family, friends, and faith leaders. These relationships provide emotional and practical reinforcement, acting as lifelines during tumultuous times. Shared prayers and communal support can solidify strength.

Faith-Filled Actions: Confront crises with actions guided by faith. These may include community involvement or helping others similarly affected, reinforcing the interconnectedness of support within your faith community.

Spiritual First-Aid Kit: Essential Faith Tools

Emergency Prayers: Simple, direct prayers act as immediate connections to divine strength. Examples include: "Jesus, be my strength in this hour of need. Grant me peace and clarity. Amen."

Anchoring Scriptures: Memorize and meditate on key scriptures for quick access in times of distress. *Psalm 46:1*: "God is our refuge and strength, an ever-present help in trouble." This assurance fosters calmness amid chaos.

Inner Reflection: Utilize moments of quiet reflection to focus your thoughts and emotions, aligning your heart with God's purposes. *Isaiah 41:10* offers reassurance: "Do not fear, for I am with you; do not be dismayed, for I am your God."

Leading Others Through Personal Trials

Modeling Faith: Demonstrate steadfastness in faith to inspire others. Your endurance through trials can serve as a powerful testament to God's sustaining power, providing encouragement to those facing similar burdens.

Encouragement and Hope: Share personal stories of overcoming obstacles through faith, encouraging others to view crises as opportunities for growth and divine timing. *2 Corinthians 1:4* emphasizes this call to comfort others "with the comfort we ourselves receive from God."

Facilitating Community Strengthening: Organize prayer groups or support networks focused on mutual encouragement, fostering resilience through collective faith and shared experiences. This creates a strong community foundation, vital during widespread crises.

Encouraging Stories: Faith at Work

Testimony of Overcoming: For example, Sarah faced a sudden cancer diagnosis that left her anxious and uncertain. However, through nightly prayer calls with her small group and constant immersion in healing scriptures, her peace returned, and her condition improved.

Hope Restored: Similarly, when Joseph's construction business went under due to a market crash, he clung to Philippians 4:19. Friends from church brought groceries, helped him network, and even pooled funds to cover essential bills until a new opportunity arose.

Wrap-Up — Courage in Crisis

Crisis times illuminate the depths of personal faith and the necessity for an adaptable, faith-driven response plan. By engaging in prayer, utilizing scripture, and fostering supportive communities, believers can navigate crises with resilience and grace. These preparatory steps create an overflow of hope and strength, transforming trials into testimonies of spiritual fortitude and divine fidelity.

In the following chapter, we will explore the lasting peace and renewed purpose found through these transformative trials, emphasizing how crises realign us with deeper understanding and spiritual insight.

Action Plan Recap

1. **Acknowledge Complete Victory in Jesus:**

- Recognize that Jesus declared "It is finished" in John 19:30, affirming that all struggles—be they physical, financial, spiritual, or emotional—have been conquered. Consistently practice gratitude, acknowledging His victory over every challenge, as expressing thankfulness attracts more blessings (1 Thessalonians 5:18).

2. **Utilize Scriptures as Anchors:**

- Regularly meditate on key Scriptures like Colossians 2:13-15, which proclaim the disarmament of all opposing spiritual forces. This mindset reinforces the understanding of the spiritual authority granted to believers over life's adversities.

3. **Engage in Proactive Faith Through Declarations:**

    - Speak life into situations by using the Word of God in prayer. Declare boldly that you are a beloved and empowered child of God. Practicing this aligns actions with faith and unleashes spiritual power, as reiterated in Proverbs 24:10 regarding the need for strength in crises.

4. Cultivate a Routine of Actionable Faith:

- Establish daily habits that strengthen faith, such as prayer, study, and declarations. Create a personal spiritual routine that includes regular application of these principles, ensuring you remain spiritually fortified and effectively leverage the complete victory Jesus has secured.

5. Navigate Crisis with Confidence in God's Plan:

- In moments of crisis, utilize collected strategies like the "spiritual first-aid kit" described in the chapter, incorporating emergency prayers and scriptures to stabilize and guide you through turbulent times. This approach builds resilience and aligns with divine assurance, fostering a journey from trials to transformative testimonies.

By integrating these steps into daily life, a believer can transition from understanding the victory of Christ to living it out consistently and fruitfully. This provides a foundation for enduring faith that thrives even amidst challenges.

CHAPTER 4

YOUR IDENTITY IN CHRIST

Your Position

Who you are is how God sees you in Christ: in Christ, you are loved, forgiven, cleansed, healed, redeemed, righteous, anointed, whole, sanctified, perfect, powerful, rich, wise, strong, honorable, glorified, blessed, and more. As you can see, you have an incredible and enviable position in Christ. This is who you are, whether you believe it or not; this is what Jesus died to make available to us.

Now that you've seen the powerful truth of your position in Christ, let's turn to something more familiar—your current reality. While your spiritual position is secure, your day-to-day experience may feel very different.

Your Current Experience

What you are experiencing right now is your reality, which for most people is far below their position in

Christ. The great question is: how do I transition from my current experience to a reality that reflects my position?

The simple answer is to become strong in the Lord and develop your faith from wherever it is to a place of great faith, strong faith, unwavering faith, genuine faith, and growing faith.

To move from your current experience to your glorious position in Christ, you must strengthen your faith and spiritual awareness. Faith is the bridge between what you see and what God has already declared to be true.

This guide will help you do both, and the process has already begun, whether you realize it or not.

7 Aspects of Your Identity

For the sake of time, we will focus on seven aspects of your identity that will most significantly impact your transformation from your current experience to your position, purchased by the Blood of Christ.

7 Aspects of Your Identity in Christ

1. I am Loved

John 3:16, John 15:9, Jeremiah 31:3: God so cherished the world that He gave His Son for us, illustrating that He loves you with the same depth, eternally and completely, as He loves the Son.

2. I am Forgiven

John 1:29, Romans 3:25, Ephesians 1:7: In Jesus, we find the ultimate sacrifice that removes the sins of the world, granting us forgiveness and releasing us from the bonds of guilt.

3. I am Redeemed

Ephesians 1:7, Galatians 3:13-14, Revelation 5:9: Through Christ, we have redemption by His blood; He bought us back from the curse and brought us into the family of God.

4. I am Righteous

Romans 5:9, 1 Corinthians 1:30, 2 Corinthians 5:21: Christ's sacrifice has justified us, making Him our righteousness so that in Him, we have become the righteousness of God.

5. I am Seated at the Right Hand of Christ

Ephesians 2:6, Colossians 1:13, Ephesians 1:3: We are not only saved but also spiritually positioned with Christ in heavenly places, sharing in His authority and blessings.

6. I am Anointed

2 Corinthians 1:21-22, Ephesians 1:13-14, Acts 10:38: God has established us in Christ and anointed us, sealing us with His Spirit and empowering us for good works.

7. I am Royalty

Revelation 1:5-6, 1 Peter 2:9, Colossians 1:13: Through His love, He has made us a kingdom of priests, a royal priesthood, called out of darkness into His wondrous light.

Embrace these truths as they reshape how you perceive your identity, fueling a transformative journey toward aligning every aspect of your life with your divine position in Christ.

Now that we've explored your identity in Christ, let's consider what empowers you to live out that identity daily: spiritual strength. It is this strength that enables you to embody your position, even in the face of life's toughest battles.

Strength

Psalm 46:1 says God is our refuge and strength. Since God is the strength of His people, what you really need is strength or God. All you and I truly need is a greater awareness of God. That's the key to recovering everything we've ever lost—and to never losing another battle ever again!

(Ps. 73:26, Isa. 41:10, Ps. 28:8-9, Ps. 29:11, Ps. 46:1, Isa. 40:31)

The purpose of this book is to help you be strong in the Lord and in the power of His might, so you can stand until you see the salvation of the Lord.

What Is Biblical Strength?

Biblical strength is the God-given ability to endure, persevere, and overcome any obstacle. It means having the courage, determination, and resilience to face whatever challenges come your way—whether they involve your health, finances, relationships, or career. This strength flows only from God and grows as you live out His Word (Joshua 1:9, Isaiah 41:10, 1 Chronicles 28:20).

Simply put, the more of the Word you have in you, the greater your strength, especially if you are a doer of the Word and not a hearer only.

For example, David faced Goliath not with physical strength but with confidence in God's power. This same inner fortitude is available to you when you rely on His Word.

Action Plan Recap

1. Embrace Your Identity in Christ

Start by truly accepting who you are in Christ. Remember, you are loved, forgiven, and redeemed. These truths form a firm foundation on which your strength and transformation are built. It's not just about knowing it—believe it deeply and let it change how you see yourself every day.

2. **Align Experience with Position**

   Aim to bring your daily experiences in line with your identity in Christ. This can mean strengthening your faith and working toward a life that reflects your spiritual truths. Our guide will help nurture the traits of great faith and resilience, ensuring your reality matches your spiritual position.

3. **Focus on Biblical Strength**

   Real strength comes from God and includes the power to endure and overcome any obstacle. Engage with the Word of God regularly, as it fuels your inner strength and empowers you to act on His will. With Scripture as your guide, you become equipped for life's challenges.

4. **Develop a Systematic Growth Plan**

   Create a personal, step-by-step plan aimed at boosting your spiritual strength. Consistent application of biblical teachings is key. Whether it's short-term improvements or long-term growth, having a plan helps direct your spiritual journey purposefully.

5. **Harness the Power of Christ**

   The power of Christ is within you, ready to help you live victoriously. Lean into this power through actions and affirmations that bolster your faith. When challenges arise, use your faith to triumph, reminding yourself that Christ's strength is your shield.

By focusing on these steps, you're not just changing habits but embracing a lifestyle that consistently aligns with your spiritual identity. It's about building a life that's both resilient and inspired by divine purpose. Keep these key points close as you move forward in your spiritual journey.

CHAPTER 5

BUILDING SPIRITUAL STRENGTH

Proverbs 24:5 says, "A wise man is strong; yes, a man of knowledge increases strength." Strength doesn't come overnight; it requires patience, focus, and consistent investment in growing your knowledge and faith.

You've already started; you're on your way, and as your day, so shall your strength be (Deuteronomy 33:25).

Stay focused.

God's Word guarantees your ever-increasing strength as you wait on Him (Isaiah 40:31).

Make the following declaration to yourself several times a day—say it in the morning and watch your days improve: "*The bolts of my gates are bronze and iron. As my day is, so is my strength. Because I am alive today, I receive strength like that of a unicorn. Today is a can-do, will-do, get-things-done day, and I am a can-do, will-do, get-things-done person. I can do all things through Christ who strengthens*

me, and I am: Deuteronomy 33:25, Psalm 92:10, Philippians 4:13."

Take Michelle, for example. She began each day with these declarations and, within weeks, noticed her confidence grow, her prayer life deepen, and her productivity increase. This simple habit of confession transformed her outlook.

Try repeating it 10, 20, or even 50 times—whatever it takes for it to sink deep into your spirit. The more you say it, the stronger your faith becomes: "***As my day is, so is my strength; my strength is like iron as long as I live.***"

Faith comes by hearing; your tongue is a fire, and you have what you say. (Romans 10:17, James 3:6, Isaiah 57:19).

Keep this in mind: you already have the essential thing you need to recover everything you have ever lost and to never lose another battle again. **It's called time.** We all have 24 hours a day. There is a quote that goes like this: **"We are all given an equal opportunity to become unequal every day."**

We have already discovered that we need strength. We have also found that God is the only reliable and dependable source of our strength. To gain more strength, therefore, you need to invest more of your time with God and in the things of God. God is a rewarder (Isaiah 45:19, Revelation 22:12, Jeremiah 17:10).

To gain more strength, we must prioritize our time with God. Ask yourself honestly: how much time have you devoted to Scripture and prayer compared to social media this week? The answer reveals the source of your current strength—and your next step toward more of it.

The benefits that Jesus obtained for us through His own obedience and sacrifice can only be maintained by our own obedience and sacrifice. There is no other way. (Luke 9:23, Luke 19:13, 1 Corinthians 15:10).

Proverbs 2:1-6, 3:1-3, 4:1-4, 7:1-3.

To grow stronger in the Lord, we must also learn how to fight effectively. God has not left us defenseless—He has given us powerful spiritual weapons designed for victory. Let's explore what they are and how to use them.

The Weapons of Our Warfare

Developing strength requires time, determination, courage, etc., but sometimes it requires tools, equipment, or weapons. For the type of battles we, as believers, must engage in, special weapons are required. The Bible refers to them as the weapons of our warfare. 2 Corinthians 10:3-5 states that the weapons of our warfare are not of this world but are mighty through God. This means they are weapons specially designed by God for victory and to strengthen us. Strength is what we need for conquest—not for the situations and circumstances confronting us to get easier.

Let me repeat: we do not need our circumstances to get easier; we need to receive grace to get stronger, better, wiser, and more obedient.

Do you know what some of these weapons are and how to apply them in your Christian walk?

The following are some of the most powerful and effective weapons in a believer's arsenal. The great news is that any one of them has proven to render the devil and his agents helpless. The combination of any two or three will always prove lethal to the enemy's camp and liberate you to enjoy the blessings obtained for us. In the next chapter, we will provide a basic understanding of who, what, why, when, where, which, and how to apply them to enhance every area of our lives. Don't limit your study to what you read here; do your homework and become more knowledgeable about each of these weapons (2 Timothy 2:15).

Check out our YouTube channel for more teaching and inspiration. It's packed with videos to help you grow stronger in your faith and apply these principles every day.

Angels

God's defensive, offensive, informational, and deliverance agents that always accompany the Word and always prevail.

(Psalm 103:20, Psalm 34:7, Exodus 23:20-33).

The Blood

God's ultimate weapon to redeem, attack, protect, safeguard, and achieve whatever Jesus has promised us.

(Revelation 13:8, Exodus 12:12-13, Revelation 12:11).

The Holy Spirit

God's chief executive officer and power source on earth.

(Acts 1:8, Zechariah 4:6, John 16:13).

The Name of Jesus

The ultimate authority in all worlds: heaven, earth, under the earth, and anywhere else.

(Mark 16:17-18, Acts 4:12, Philippians 2:9-11).

The Word

The substance from which all weapons are made.

(John 1:1, Hebrews 1:2-3, Psalm 33:6).

Prayer, Praise, and Worship

Give us direct access to God and bring God on the scene on demand. (Psalm 16:11, 2 Chronicles 20:22, Acts 16:25-26).

The Holy Communion

Helps us tap into all the graces that Jesus obtained for us and manifested in His

life. (1 Corinthians 11:23-26, Matthew 26:26-29, Luke 22:19-20).

The Anointing Oil

Affirms your kingship and royal destiny. (1 Samuel 10:1-2, 6 & 9, 2 Corinthians 1:20-22, Isaiah 45:1-3).

Sacrifice and Service

Guarantee corresponding blessings.

(Matthew 6:33, Exodus 23:25-26, Mark 10:29-30).

Action Plan Recap

1. **Invest Time Wisely**: Recognize the critical role time plays in developing spiritual strength. Allocate substantial daily time to engage with God and invest in Scripture study, which enhances your resilience and faith.

2. **Make Daily Declarations**: Strengthen your mindset and spiritual fortitude with consistent affirmations. Declare positive and empowering statements each morning, reinforcing your belief in achieving all tasks through Christ's strength.

3. **Balance Technology Use**: Evaluate how your time spent on social media compares with time dedicated to spiritual growth. Strive for a healthy

balance by reducing screen time and increasing engagement with spiritual practices for enhanced strength.

4. **Utilize Spiritual Weapons**: Familiarize yourself with the spiritual weapons at your disposal, like the Word of God, prayer, and the Holy Spirit. Learn how to effectively deploy these weapons to fortify yourself against spiritual challenges.

5. **Develop a Personal Growth Plan**: Create a systematic plan for spiritual development, comprising short (7-day), medium (30 and 90 days), and long-term (1-year) goals. Use these plans to track progress and enhance your spiritual strength over time.

CHAPTER 6

POWER OF ANGELS

Who Are Angels?

Angels are God's powerful messengers who serve Him faithfully (Luke 1:11–13; Revelation 1:1). They accompany the King of Kings by the thousands—millions, even (Psalm 68:17; Revelation 19:14). Because there are always enough angels to carry out God's commands, we can trust that His word never returns void (Isaiah 55:11). When you speak His word with boldness, angels are ready to act on it (Psalm 103:20).

What Do Angels Do?

Angels minister to God's children. In other words, angels carry out God's Word and messages for the benefit of His children—those of us who believe in Jesus and are heirs of salvation. Angels execute every instruction God has given in the Bible concerning us (Hebrews 1:14).

How Powerful Are Angels?

Angels are so powerful that one angel is said to have killed 185,000 Assyrian soldiers in one day (2 Kings 19:35; Isaiah 37:36; 2 Chronicles 32:21). Angels represent the voice of the LORD (Isaiah 30:31).

In Matthew 26:53, Jesus says He could have called more than twelve legions of angels. A legion, historically, refers to 3,000–6,000 Roman soldiers—meaning Jesus was speaking of 36,000 to 72,000 angels at His command! That's an astounding measure of divine power available to you and me.

Do you realize how much power and resources are available to us through angels alone, not to mention other spiritual weapons?

How Do I Engage the Ministry of Angels in My Life?

Engaging the ministry of angels can be a transformative experience in a believer's life. Here are three principal methods to effectively activate angelic presence and intervention.

1. Voice Activation

Purpose: Engage angels through vocalizing God's Word.

Angels respond to God's Word, as stated in *Psalm* 103:20, where it is affirmed that angels are attentive to His commands. By speaking scripture aloud, you align your words with God's authority, granting angels the right to act on your behalf. For example, when you declare scriptures like "By Jesus's stripes I am healed" (1 Peter 2:24) in faith, angels recognize it as God's command and go to work. However, if you say, "I feel so sick," angels remain inactive—it's not the Lord's word. Worse, negative words can empower demonic forces (John 8:44; Revelation 12:9). Always speak what is written—just as Jesus did in Matthew *(Matthew 4:4, 4:7,* 4:10) to keep yourself aligned with heaven.

2. Prayer and Fasting

Purpose: Encourage angelic intervention through devoted spiritual discipline.

Prayer and fasting are powerful tools for provoking angelic assistance. As exemplified in *Matthew* 4:11, after Jesus fasted and resisted the devil using scripture, angels came to minister to Him. Regular fasting, such as skipping one or more meals a week, can open avenues for spiritual and angelic interactions. Consider how Cornelius's consistent prayers and fasting resulted in an angelic visitation *(Acts* 10:30), or how fasting rescued Paul from peril *(Acts* 27:20-23). Establish a regular fasting schedule, prioritizing spiritual readiness as shown in *Luke 18:12* and *Matthew* 6:17.

3. The Fear of the LORD

Purpose: Develop a deep reverence that aligns you with divine presence.

Walking in the reverential fear of the Lord invites angelic engagement. *Psalm 34:7* states that the angel of the Lord encamps around those who fear Him. Cornelius, noted for his devout nature, received divine revelation due to his godliness *(Acts 10:2)*. Similarly, Daniel's prayers and reverence brought him visions from Gabriel *(Daniel 9:3 & 20-23)*. Living with awe and respect enhances openness to angelic ministry.

By adopting these methods, you invite a more pronounced and active angelic presence into your life. Integrating the right spiritual disciplines aligned with divine principles ensures a robust and supportive relationship with these heavenly beings.

Additional Ways Angels Can Help You

1. **Angels and Your All-Around Blessings (Exodus 23:20-33):** Just as God sent an angel to guide and protect the Israelites on their journey, angels are present in your life to direct you towards paths of blessing and abundance.

2. **Angels and Your Health (John 5:1-4):** Just like the angel at the pool of Bethesda who stirred the waters for healing, angels today can be a divine assistance in ministering health, aligning with God's will.

3. **Angels and Your Protection (Psalm 91:10-11):** As promised, angels guard you from harm, encircling you with divine protection and ensuring safety through life's challenges.

4. **Angels and Your Deliverance (Acts 12:5-10):** Peter's miraculous escape from prison through angelic intervention is a reminder that angels can facilitate your deliverance from difficult and seemingly impossible situations and habits.

5. **Angels and Your Provision (1 Kings 19:3-8):** Like the angel who provided Elijah with sustenance, angels can assist in ensuring that your needs are met, bringing miraculous provision when it's needed the most.

6. **Angels and Your Strength/Encouragement (Luke 22:41-43):** Just as an angel strengthened Jesus in His time of need, angels offer support and encouragement to bolster your spirit during challenging times.

Action Plan Recap

1. **Understand the Role of Angels:** Recognize angels as powerful messengers and ministers for God's children. They can execute God's Word and support believers in spiritual battles.

2. **Activate Angels Through God's Word:** Learn to engage angels by voicing God's Word in faith. Speaking scriptures activates angelic intervention by aligning your words with divine authority, empowering angels to act on your behalf.

3. **Incorporate Prayer and Fasting:** Establish a regular schedule for prayer and fasting. This spiritual discipline is a proven method to provoke angelic assistance and bolster your spiritual strength.

4. **Embrace the Fear of the Lord:** Foster a lifestyle marked by reverential fear of the Lord. Walking in His ways invites divine protection and angelic support, as seen in biblical examples.

5. **Explore Angelic Assistance in Various Aspects:** Identify ways angels can enhance your life, such as providing protection, health support, deliverance, and peace. Utilize these divine resources by studying relevant scriptures and applying the insights to your spiritual journey.

CHAPTER 7

THE POWER OF THE BLOOD

Introduction: What Is the Blood of Jesus?

The Blood of Jesus is, without question, the most powerful and consequential weapon in the believer's arsenal. While every spiritual weapon has divine authority when properly engaged, the Blood stands apart—it is foundational, indispensable, and eternally effective.

Before The Foundation of The World

The concept of God's pre-planned redemptive policy reflects divine foresight and love, ensuring humanity's safety even before creation. This coverage can be understood in three transformative steps:

1. **Creation**

    Genesis 1:1 highlights the inception of the universe, a testament to God's supreme intention in crafting a world that mirrors His glory. By Genesis

1:26-28, humanity is created in God's image, designated for dominion and fellowship, epitomizing divine craftsmanship.

2. Foreknowledge of Man's Fall

Anticipating the potential downfall instigated by Satan, God's plan accounted for humanity's vulnerabilities. His foresight is proactive rather than reactionary, as evidenced by Revelation 13:8, Ephesians 1:4, and 1 Peter 1:19-20, which point to a predestined solution established before the foundation of the world. This solution is embodied in Christ's sacrificial atonement, encompassing all conceivable failings.

3. Establishment of the Eternal Policy: The Blood of Jesus

This divine insurance policy, symbolized by Christ's blood, secures humanity's redemption. It promises restoration and eternal security, ensuring that God's grace covers all sins and guarantees eternal life—preparations made millennia before humanity's need arose.

Through these steps, the narrative of God's preemptive love and majesty is not only preserved but clarified, revealing a God who prepared a pathway back to Himself even before the first act of creation. The timelessness of this plan underscores God's enduring commitment to humanity, offering comfort and assurance that His grace pre-existed our need for it.

It's Time to File a Claim Against the Eternal Life Policy.

Will The Policy Pay?

In Genesis 3:1-7, the serpent, Satan—the deceiver who, as stated in Revelation 12:9, became the dragon—deceived Adam and Eve, disrupting the Divine order. Their eyes were opened to the myriad issues now plaguing mankind: fear, doubt, worry, anxiety, depression, oppression, sickness, disease, lack, scarcity, poverty, loneliness—whatever problems, issues, or challenges you can name or imagine came into existence because Adam and Eve listened to the devil, who deceived them and stole their original God-given birthright.

They realized they were naked and exposed, necessitating some form of coverage or insurance policy. They created a temporary solution, known as the fig leaves policy, which was inadequate because leaves dry up once removed from the ground or tree (Genesis 3:7).

When they heard the voice of God in the Garden, they hid from His presence. Since then, mankind has been hiding from one thing or another. God asked them where they were; Adam replied, "I heard Your voice and was afraid because I was naked; so, I hid myself" (Genesis 3:8-11).

The First Application of Blood for Atonement in the Bible

To summarize, God realized that the Eternal Life Insurance Policy He had established would need to be activated, but certain conditions had to be met, which would take approximately 4,000 years from the days of Adam and Eve. In Genesis 3:20-21, God presented His insurance policy as a down payment to atone for Adam and Eve's sin, based on His foreknowledge according to Revelation 13:8. He made coats of skin and clothed them.

Consider this: what must happen before you can access the skin of any animal? The answer is that you must shed the blood of the animal. This is the first reference to blood in the Bible, with the first mention occurring in Genesis 4:10. A sacrifice is required; this bloodshed foreshadows the blood of Jesus that will ultimately redeem humanity (1 Corinthians 5:7).

This is a much better solution than fig leaves, but it does not constitute the policy itself. The redemption of man required the blood of a perfect man.

With the fall of man in Genesis 3:7, sin entered the world, introducing all the issues that humanity has faced ever since: fear, lack, sickness, oppression, depression, relationship problems, etc. All these issues became illegal in John 19:30. At Calvary, He didn't whisper—He declared: "It is finished!" That declaration legally canceled every curse and every deficit. Therefore, when you receive Jesus as your Lord and Savior by putting your faith in His blood, all these things become automatically illegal in your life as well. This book is about legally and scripturally evicting them out of your life. Read on.

All the issues and problems of mankind are derivatives of sin. That is why John the Baptist called Jesus the Lamb of God who takes away the sin of the world (John 1:29). Where there is no sin, there can be no lack, sickness, disease, oppression, or depression. By applying the blood of Jesus, you're serving a divine notice to every illegal spiritual activity in your life.

Escape from Egypt (Bondage and All Kinds of Problems) By The Blood

Just as the blood covered Adam and Eve after their fall, another pivotal moment occurred generations later in Egypt—when the Israelites needed divine coverage again. The eternal policy was echoed in the Passover lamb, a foreshadowing of Christ's ultimate sacrifice. After over 430 years of captivity in Egypt, it was time to set them free, but nothing could accomplish this except the blood. I declare that you too are coming out of every form of wickedness holding you captive in any area of your life by the Blood of Jesus. Pray like this: **"By the Blood of Jesus, I decree my liberty and freedom from every activity or operation of the devil that has held me captive in the Name of Jesus."**

After Egypt suffered plague after plague, Pharaoh was indecisive. The Israelites were filled with hope and despair, dreaming of freedom but never being let go permanently. Perhaps you have had similar experiences—practicing one spiritual discipline or another, going to church, fasting, evangelizing, giving, serving, attending night vigils, engaging in warfare prayer, etc. Despite your efforts, it may feel like you take two steps forward and three steps back. That's likely how the Israelites felt, thinking, "We've been here for over 400 years; nothing is going to change." Generational bondage can feel inescapable. Your situation might be different—perhaps illness, family issues with marriage, employment problems, or financial struggles. Whatever prevents you from feeling free and blessed is a form of bondage. The good news is that Galatians 5:1 and John 8:36 both proclaim that whom the Son sets free is truly free. Pharaoh thought he was tough and a match for God, just as the forces harassing you now may believe they will always have the upper hand. God had news for Pharaoh, and He has news for the powers, principalities, rulers of darkness, and spiritual wickedness troubling you: their time is up, by the authority of the blood of the everlasting covenant.

Enough Is Enough

In Exodus 11:1, God declared that enough is enough regarding His people's suffering. He is the God of all the earth, the King of kings and the LORD of lords, almighty and the Highest God. He is the mighty Man in battle, your Savior and Deliverer, your refuge and fortress, your shield and glory, and the lifter of your head. You have suffered enough, and He has come to lift you up (Leviticus 26:13). Get ready and stay ready; it's blood time. When the blood shows up, the Egyptians you see today, along with all your other problems, issues, and challenges, must give way. They must bow and surrender because there was a policy issued to cover all your problems before the foundation of the world (Revelation 13:8). God is not presenting the policy now; the time is not yet. The Real Lamb of God has not yet been presented (John 1:29; 1 Corinthians 5:7). For now, I will introduce a sample—a photocopy of the policy—and based on that, Pharaoh will let you go (Exodus 11:1). Please read Exodus chapters 11 and 12 at least three times to gain a full understanding of this subject.

It's Time to Pass Over All Problems and Issues You No Longer Desire.

In Exodus 12:1-24, God instructed Moses on the Passover, where the Passover lamb was introduced as a down payment for the Real Lamb yet to come (John 1:29; 1 Corinthians 5:7; Revelation 13:8). At midnight as it was in Egypt, it is going down for you too—not tomorrow, but today. (Today, Not Tomorrow)

The Midnight Mission

In Exodus 12:12-13, God reveals some benefits of applying the blood: a) the destruction of all the firstborn in the land of Egypt (symbolizing the powers and demonic forces causing you problems), and b) the execution of judgment against the gods of the land (indicating that the authorities behind the demons troubling you will also be dealt with).

In verse 13, c) the blood will be a token upon your houses, which also applies to all your belongings, possessions, affairs, and household. According to Hebrews 9:22, God says that when He sees the blood, which serves as a token or sign upon your houses or anything belonging to you, He will pass over you and yours when He destroys all your enemies and opposition. Pray like this:

"I cover myself with the Blood of Jesus; therefore, any evil targeted against me, my family, my belongings, my possessions, my work, my name and identity, including all my affairs, must pass over, in the Name of Jesus." Make this declaration several times a day, every day.

In Exodus 12:22-24, God gives Moses instructions on how to apply the shed blood of the lamb. Pay very close attention, as you are about to learn specifics about how to apply the blood in your life—not the blood of bulls and goats, but the Precious Blood of Jesus. Remember that Exodus 12 is a foreshadowing of what happened at Calvary. 1 Corinthians 5:7 states that Christ, our Passover, is sacrificed for us.

Verse 22 says, "And ye shall take a bunch of hyssop and dip it in the blood that is in the bason and strike the lintel and the two side posts with the blood that is in the bason...". The blood of the lamb that was shed was placed in the bason.

1 Corinthians 5:7 tells us that the blood of Jesus has been shed and presented in heaven, in the Holiest of all (Hebrews 9:3-7).

Thus, the purpose of the hyssop is to transport the blood from the bason to the lintel and side posts—essentially moving the blood from where it has been presented to where it is to be applied. In our context, this means from the Holiest of all to your finances, your health, your relationships, your employment, etc.

What, in your understanding of the Bible, is the transporting agent (hyssop) for born-again believers? We will return to that shortly; for now, let's learn more about hyssop.

What is Hyssop?

Hyssop is a plant used in the Bible for ritual cleansing and purification. It symbolizes spiritual cleansing and God's unmerited grace. Biblical examples of hyssop's use include cleansing (Psalm 51:7) and the Passover rituals (John 19:29), as well as sprinkling (Hebrews 9:19).

Hyssop is known to be an expectorant, aiding respiratory health by helping to clear the airways and soften mucus.

It is also recognized for its carminative qualities, which assist with digestive health.

Additionally, hyssop possesses antimicrobial and anti-inflammatory properties that help combat infections.

It is furthermore believed to have antioxidant and anti-cancer properties. These qualities point not only to physical healing and purification but also serve as metaphors for spiritual renewal. Just as hyssop clears physical impurities, our confessions—rooted in God's Word—clear the way for divine intervention.

With all these properties of hyssop, it is no surprise that God would use such a plant to maintain the purity of the blood as it travels from the bason to the lintel, or from where it is preserved to the problem area.

What Is the Believer's Hyssop?

Returning to my earlier question: What, in your understanding of the Bible, is the transporting agent (hyssop) for born-again believers today?

The answer is simple: it is your mouth, your tongue, your lips (Revelation 12:11, Job 22:28, Isaiah 57:19). According to Genesis 2:7 (Chumash translation), you are a speaking spirit. Do you remember the first time you applied the blood in your life? Your first encounter with applying the blood of Jesus likely occurred when you gave your life to Christ. You believed in your heart that Jesus died for your sins by shedding His blood on the cross (Romans 3:25-27). He was buried and rose again from the dead. You put your faith in the blood and confessed with your mouth (Romans 10:9-10).

"For with the heart man believeth unto righteousness (achieved by faith in the blood), and with the mouth confession is made unto salvation" (Romans 10:10).

To put it another way, with your heart, you believe in the shed blood of Jesus, presented in the Holiest of all (heavenly bason, Hebrews 9:12), and with your tongue—the hyssop—confession is made unto salvation, sound health, financial abundance, a happy home life, great employment, joy unspeakable, peace of God, and solutions to any and every problem you might face. Remember what Jesus said in John 19:30: all your problems have been solved. You are restored to the Garden with the Holy Spirit in you for character development and upon you for conquest and exploits. The first time the Spirit of God entered man, he became a speaking spirit. Sin changed everything in Genesis chapter 3. Adam and Eve opted for fig leaves therapy, which did not work and never works. Without the shedding of blood, there is no remission of sins, so God intervened and covered them with coats of skin, meaning blood was shed, but it was not the blood of the Lamb that was slain before the foundation of the world (Revelation 13:8)—that had to wait. The patriarchs Abraham, Isaac, and Jacob all offered blood to atone for their sins. Moses introduced the Israelite community to this in Exodus 11 and 12. Job, King

Saul, King David, King Solomon, and many Old Testament figures applied the blood as a means of atonement.

Then came Jesus (John 1:29), the real deal. He shed His blood and completely removed sin once and for all (Hebrews 9:6-13) and declared, "It is finished" (John 19:30). So, start speaking and applying the blood of Jesus to every area of need and concern in your life. You're all set—open wide your mouth, and God will fill it (Psalm 81:10-14; Luke 21:15; Jeremiah 1:12).

Stay Focused Until the Morning

Returning to the last part of Exodus 12:22: "And none of you shall go out at the door of his house until the morning."

What does this portion of the text mean? Now that you understand what the blood is and what it can do, remember that the blood atones, protects, delivers, heals, prospers, makes righteous, sanctifies, destroys curses, and blesses in every way the Bible promises. You know how to transport it from the bason (the presence of God) to solve your problems using the hyssop (your mouth).

Once you do that, you must continue saying and affirming your deliverance until morning. Recall that all this began at midnight (the time of problems). You must keep the blood applied by holding fast to your confession of faith with thanksgiving until morning (the solution to your problems) (Hebrews 3:1; 10:23;

10:35-39). It takes faith to apply the blood, and it will require faith to walk and stand by that faith until morning (2 Corinthians 5:7; Romans 5:2).

Exodus 12:24 is instructive because it explains why many believers do not experience the results of what the blood of Jesus has obtained for us. Simply put, it is a lack of application. There is a saying that goes: **"Your life will not change because you know what to do; your life will change when you do what you know to do."** This quote is attributed to Dr. Robert Anthony.

God is not a respecter of persons; He is only a respecter of His Word. Verse 23 states that God will destroy the wicked, but when He sees the blood applied to your house, family, belongings, etc., He will pass over you and will not allow the destroyer to enter your houses to smite you. This means you can know about the blood, honor the blood, and even tell others about the blood, but unless you open your mouth and apply it to the areas of your life where you need help, the blood will not benefit you. It is akin to someone who knows Jesus died for their sins but refuses to confess with their mouth what they believe in their heart; that person will remain unsaved. You must open your mouth and declare your salvation, abundance, health, peace, joy, and more.

How often should you do it? Continue until you see the results you are striving for. Once that is accomplished, move on to the next area of interest or concern, and keep doing this indefinitely. That's what Exodus 12:25 says.

Seven Additional Ways the Blood Can Bless You

The Blood and Your All-Around Blessings – Revelation 5:12: Through the blood of Jesus, receive blessings of power, wealth, wisdom, strength, honor, glory, and praise, enriching every aspect of your life.

The Blood and Your Health – 1 Peter 2:24: As Jesus bore our sins, by His wounds, we are healed; the Blood provides divine health and wholeness when applied with faith.

The Blood and Your Spiritual Warfare – Revelation 12:11: Overcome adversaries, habits, addictions and spiritual battles by the blood of the Lamb and the word of testimony, a powerful duo securing victory in spiritual warfare.

The Blood and Your Deliverance – Exodus 12:12-13: Just as the Israelites found protection and escape through the Passover blood, the Blood of Jesus offers deliverance and safety from all forms of bondage.

The Blood and Your Provision/Riches – 2 Corinthians 8:9: Despite Christ's richness, He became poor for our sake, so that through His poverty, we might become rich, ensuring divine provision through His sacrifice.

The Blood and Your Strength/Encouragement – Hebrews 10:19: By the Blood, draw near to God with boldness; it serves as a source of encouragement and spiritual fortitude, empowering believers to stand firm.

The Blood and Your Peace – Colossians 1:19-20: The Blood of Christ reconciles all things, creating peace and unifying divides, providing tranquility that surpasses understanding.

Sharon's Story

To illustrate this powerful truth, let's consider a real-world example. Sharon's testimony shows how applying the blood of Jesus—through confession, fasting, and prayer—can lead to miraculous transformation. Amid life's daunting challenges, Sharon found herself at a crossroads that tested her faith like never before. Living in a small town, she had always considered herself devout, but what she was about to face would push her spiritual boundaries further than she anticipated. Her business, once thriving, was facing severe financial strain. Bills mounted, and the prospects seemed dim. Moreover, her once vibrant health began to suffer inexplicably, leaving her increasingly desperate for a breakthrough.

Realizing the gravity of her situation, Sharon turned to the spiritual teachings she had embraced but never fully applied. She discovered that her struggle was a battle requiring more than passive hope; it demanded active faith and engagement with the spiritual weapons she had read about but often overlooked. Prompted by a sermon that spoke on the power of *fasting* and the *blood of* Jesus, Sharon decided it was time to employ these tools wholeheartedly.

She embarked on a structured period of fasting, choosing to replace certain meals with dedicated prayer time. These were not just prayers of desperation but declarations, using specific scriptural promises to reinforce her trust in divine intervention. During this period, Sharon continually proclaimed the power of the blood of Jesus over her circumstances, visualizing its protective and redemptive power flowing into every corner of her life.

As days turned into weeks, Sharon noticed subtle yet profound changes. Her health, which had baffled doctors, began to stabilize. More astonishingly, her business received unexpected opportunities—clients who had long delayed payments suddenly cleared their dues, and new prospects emerged, seemingly out of nowhere.

Sharon's experience was not just a series of fortunate events; it was the culmination of a strategic spiritual offensive. By combining fasting—a means of drawing closer to God and sharpening her spiritual focus—with claiming the blood of Jesus—symbolizing the ultimate victory over all adversities—Sharon triumphed over her crises. It reinforced her belief that these spiritual disciplines were not just antiquated practices but vital components of a victory strategy.

Through Sharon's journey, she not only regained her footing but discovered a new depth in her faith. Her story became a beacon to others in her community, illustrating the transformative power that lies in spiritual discipline when faced with life's fiercest storms. Sharon's testimony of deliverance became a living testament to the power and victory available to every believer willing to engage fully with the divine arsenal provided through faith.

Blood Activation Checklist

Your Homework:

- Recognize Redemption: Remember, Jesus's Blood was shed to resolve every issue you face today. His victory was sealed over 2,000 years ago (John 19:30).

- Pinpoint Focus Areas: Choose three areas in your life needing transformation. Create intentional prayer points centered on these areas.

- Resources and Growth: Join our Tuesday Night Prayer and Bible Study on Facebook Live to deepen your understanding. Consider reading *The Fundamentals of The Blood of Jesus* for practical applications and further insight into leveraging Christ's redemptive power.

Action Plan Recap:

1. Understand the Blood's Power

   Recognize the blood of Jesus as the cornerstone of both spiritual warfare and eternal assurance—it's God's ultimate life insurance policy (Leviticus 17:11, Hebrews 9:22).

2. Apply it Daily with Your Voice (Your Hyssop)

   Develop a habit of declaring the blood's power over all areas of your life. Use spoken words to apply its protection and redemption daily (Revelation 12:11, Romans 10:10).

3. Stay Focused and Consistent

   Maintain steady faith by regularly affirming the blood's power in your life, especially in challenging times, to usher in 'morning' solutions (Exodus 12:22).

4. Plead/Apply the Blood in Warfare Prayers

   Just as the Israelites used the Passover blood for protection, fervently plead the blood over life's challenges for breakthrough and deliverance (Exodus 12:12-13).

5. Stay Connected to Teaching and Fellow Believers

   Join study groups emphasizing the blood's spiritual significance. This bolsters understanding and promotes spiritual growth within a supportive community.

By faithfully enacting this checklist, you harness the transformative might of the blood of Jesus, equipping yourself to confidently navigate and conquer spiritual battles.

CHAPTER 8

THE POWER OF THE HOLY SPIRIT

Now that we've seen the unmatched power of the Blood, let's turn to the next divine agent in our supernatural arsenal: the Holy Spirit. While the Blood redeems, protects, and establishes covenant, the Holy Spirit fills, leads, and empowers. In this chapter, we'll explore how the Spirit equips believers for victorious living—every day, in every battle.

Understanding the Role of the Holy Spirit in Your Life

1. Who Is the Holy Spirit?

The Holy Spirit, recognized as the third person of the Trinity, represents God's divine essence actively involved in the lives of believers. His multifaceted roles underscore His dynamic presence:

- The Spirit of God (Genesis 1:2): From creation, the Spirit of God hovered over the waters, symbolizing creative power and divine order.

- The Comforter (John 14:26): As our advocate, He comforts and assures us, reminding believers of Christ's teachings, providing peace and assurance in times of need.

- The Spirit of Truth (John 16:13): The Holy Spirit leads us into all truth, revealing God's wisdom and helping us discern His will amidst life's complexities.

The Spirit of Power (Acts 1:8): Endows believers with the power to witness boldly, equipping them for ministry and life's mission.

With this understanding of who the Holy Spirit is, we can now explore what He accomplishes in a believer's life.

2. What the Holy Spirit Can Do Through You

The Holy Spirit fulfills numerous vital roles that facilitate internal growth and spiritual vitality:

- **Teaches and Guides (John 16:13):** Acts as a divine teacher and guide, illuminating God's word and ways. He ensures we navigate daily life with wisdom anchored in spiritual truths.

- **Empowers for Miracles (Acts 1:8):** Provides the extraordinary ability to perform miracles, giving believers the strength to manifest God's power in tangible ways.

- **Convicts of Sin (John 16:8):** Brings an awareness of sin, righteousness, and judgment, leading to repentance and a deeper relationship with God.

- **Intercedes for Us (Romans 8:26):** Engages in prayer on our behalf with groans too deep for words, supporting us in our weaknesses and guiding us through life's challenges.

  Beyond general empowerment, the Holy Spirit also played a pivotal role in Jesus' ministry, highlighting the model He set for us.

3. Unlocking the Spirit's Power in Your Life

The Holy Spirit is immensely powerful, influencing all aspects of creation and resurrection, testifying to His divine majesty:

- **Acts 1:8:** Empowers believers, enabling them to witness courageously and faithfully across the world.
- **Genesis 1:2:** Played a crucial role in creation, demonstrating dynamic involvement and power in shaping the universe.
- **Romans 8:11:** The same Spirit who resurrected Jesus imparts life to our mortal bodies, showcasing His transformative and life-giving power.

  With a grasp of this power, consider how you can engage with the Holy Spirit in daily life.

4. How Do I Engage the Ministry of the Holy Spirit?

Engaging the Holy Spirit is essential for a vibrant and effective spiritual life. Here's how:

- **Invite Him Daily (Luke 11:13):** Open your heart to His influence every day, inviting Him to lead and transform your life.
- **Listen to His Voice (John 10:27):** Cultivate a practice of listening and responding to His gentle guidance amidst life's noise.
- **Walk in His Power (Galatians 5:16):** Allow His strength to guide your actions, living by the Spirit to overcome carnal challenges.
- **Pray in the Spirit (Jude 1:20):** Strengthen your spiritual foundation through intuitive communication, fostering a closer connection with God.

  We now examine how the Spirit enriched the life and work of Jesus, providing a blueprint for our own spiritual journey.

5. The Holy Spirit in the Life of Jesus

The Holy Spirit significantly influenced Jesus' life on earth, showing us the way to live:

- **Luke 1:35:** Initiated Jesus' earthly presence through divine conception, signifying His holy mission from birth.
- **Matthew 3:16:** Anointed Jesus at His baptism, marking the commencement of His public ministry with divine validation and strength.
- **Luke 4:1:** Guided Jesus into the wilderness, emphasizing trust and dependence on God's direction.

- **Luke 4:18:** Empowered Jesus to preach, heal, and deliver, manifesting God's kingdom on earth through acts of compassion and power.

With this foundation, reflect on how the Holy Spirit supports health in believers today.

6. The Holy Spirit and Your Health

The Spirit cares for our physical and spiritual well-being, reinforcing health and vitality:

- **Romans 8:11:** The Spirit imparts divine vigor to our bodies, renewing and sustaining our physical existence through God's power.
- **1 Corinthians 6:19-20:** Our bodies, being His temple, are treated with reverence and care, imbued with divine purpose and wellness.
- **Isaiah 53:5:** His healing presence actualizes the promise of health through Christ's sacrifice, enforcing divine healing effectively.

Beyond health, let's look into the ways the Spirit safeguards us in spiritual battles.

7. The Holy Spirit and Your Protection (Spiritual Warfare)

The Holy Spirit equips and fortifies us against spiritual adversities:

- **Ephesians 6:17:** Acts as our defense and offensive power by allowing us to wield the Word, protecting us from spiritual threats.

- **Isaiah 59:19:** Raises a standard against enemy onslaughts, ensuring we remain standing amidst battles.
- **Romans 8:26:** His intercession provides strength and guidance, supporting us in struggles beyond human capability.

Protection assured, consider how deliverance is facilitated through the Spirit.

8. The Holy Spirit and Your Deliverance

The Holy Spirit actively liberates and frees believers from bondage:

- **Isaiah 10:27:** Breaks yokes through the Spirit's anointing, liberating us from oppressive spiritual chains.
- **Luke 4:18:** Continues the liberation mission Jesus began, freeing captives and proclaiming release to the downtrodden.

Beyond deliverance, the Spirit also ensures provision and sustenance in times of need.

9. The Holy Spirit and Your Provision

Beyond spiritual needs, the Holy Spirit ensures divine provision:

- **John 16:15:** Reveals God's abundant resources and ensures we access divine insight and guidance.

- **1 Kings 17:14-16:** Like Elijah's provision, He orchestrates sustenance, demonstrating God's ability to intervene supernaturally in our scarcity.

When faced with challenges, the Spirit provides strength and encouragement.

10. The Holy Spirit and Your Strength/Encouragement

In times of need, the Spirit infuses us with courage and resilience:

- **Nehemiah 8:10:** His joy becomes our strength, sustaining us through difficult moments with divine encouragement.
- **Romans 15:13:** Fills us with hope and inner strength, equipping us to flourish and persevere.
- **Isaiah 40:31:** Renews our strength, enabling us to soar above life's challenges and heartaches.

Finally, the Holy Spirit brings peace, a calming assurance that transcends turmoil.

11. Receiving Supernatural Peace Through the Spirit

Experience tranquility and assurance through the Holy Spirit:

- **John 14:26-27:** Offers peace and comfort, assuring hearts troubled by life's uncertainties.

Romans 8:6 provides spiritual tranquility, cultivating a mind governed by life and peace.

- Philippians 4:7 assures us that His peace, far beyond understanding, safeguards our hearts and minds, fostering serenity.

These insights into the Holy Spirit's work underscore His invaluable presence in nurturing, guiding, and empowering believers, facilitating a rich, faith-filled life in harmony with God's divine will.

FINAL DECLARATION: WALKING IN VICTORY

Use this declaration daily, but feel free to tailor it to the specific battles you are facing right now. Your words matter.

"Father, in the name of Jesus, I receive the full power of the Holy Spirit. I stand in divine authority over every sickness, lack, fear, and oppression. I declare health, provision, strength, and peace over my life. Holy Spirit, guide me, empower me, and protect me. I walk in supernatural victory, in Jesus' mighty name! Amen!"

Now take a moment to speak your own words. What battles are you facing today? Declare the Spirit's power and presence over those areas with bold faith.

Action Plan Recap

To live in daily supernatural victory, you must engage the Holy Spirit intentionally and consistently. This action plan summarizes how to make His presence a practical reality in every area of your life.

1. **Daily Invitation and Engagement**: Actively invite the Holy Spirit into your daily life through prayer (Luke 11:13). Make it a habit to consciously seek His guidance and empowerment each day.

2. **Learn and Listen**: Cultivate an attentive spirit by listening to the Holy Spirit's guidance (John 10:27). Engage in practices that help you discern His voice, such as meditating on scripture and reflecting.

3. **Walk in His Power**: Apply the power of the Holy Spirit in your actions by aligning your life with biblical principles. This includes making decisions and taking actions that reflect His teachings and the empowerment He provides (Galatians 5:16).

4. **Prayer and Intercession**: Develop a habit of praying in the Spirit (Jude 1:20). This spiritual discipline strengthens your faith and helps you rely on the Holy Spirit for intercession and guidance in your spiritual warfare.

5. **Utilize the Holy Spirit for Protection and Deliverance**: Trust in the Holy Spirit's role in protecting you from spiritual adversities (Ephesians 6:17) and breaking yokes (Isaiah 10:27). Use prayer and

scriptural affirmations as tools to harness His protective and delivering power.

By integrating these steps into your spiritual practice, you can effectively engage the Holy Spirit.

CHAPTER 9

POWER IN JESUS'S NAME

Have you ever spoken a name and watched a situation shift? The name of Jesus isn't just sacred—it's powerful. In this chapter, you'll discover what makes His name unlike any other.

1. What Does "Name" Mean?

In biblical terms, a **name** represents a person's identity, authority, and destiny. In ancient Hebrew culture, names were deeply significant, often reflecting a person's character or purpose.

- **In the natural world**, a name identifies and distinguishes an individual.

- **In the spiritual world**, a name carries authority and power.

The name "**Jesus**" comes from the Hebrew name **Yeshua**, meaning **"Yahweh (God) saves"** or **"The Lord is Salvation"** (Matthew 1:21). His name is not just a title; it reveals His mission to save, heal, deliver, and establish God's kingdom.

2. How Did Jesus Obtain His Name?

The name of Jesus was not randomly given; He received it by **divine appointment** and **heavenly authority**.

Three Ways Jesus Obtained His Name:

The name of Jesus was conferred upon Him through divine means, reflecting unparalleled authority and eternal significance. This occurred through three distinct modes: inheritance, bestowal, and conquest. Here's how each uniquely contributes to His name:

1. By Inheritance

Pre-existence and Identity: As the eternal Son of God, Jesus's name was inherited from the Father. According to *Hebrews 1:4*, He has "inherited a name more excellent than the angels," signifying His divine nature and preeminence above all creation. This inheritance is not merely a title; it reflects His inherent identity as the divine Son, establishing His eternal authority and unmatched status.

2. By Bestowal

Post-Resurrection Exaltation: Following His earthly ministry and ultimate sacrifice, God the Father exalted Jesus, bestowing upon Him the name above all names as stated in *Philippians 2:9-11*. This bestowal represents God's recognition of Jesus's obedience and sacrifice, honoring Him with exaltation above every being in heaven and earth. This act signifies both divine endorsement and acknowledgment of Jesus's role in God's redemptive plan.

3. By Conquest

Victory Through the Cross: Jesus's victory over sin, death, and the forces of evil secured His name through conquest. In *Colossians 2:15*, it is proclaimed that Jesus "disarmed the rulers and authorities and made a public spectacle of them." This conquest affirms His triumph over all spiritual adversaries, solidifying His name as powerful and victorious, recognized even in the spiritual realms.

Each mode is deeply grounded in scripture and theology, not simply poetic ideas. Together, they affirm Jesus's comprehensive authority and the powerful legacy of His name, encompassing divine inheritance, bestowed honor, and conclusive victory. These facets form a complete picture of why Jesus's name holds ultimate significance and the power to transform lives.

3. How Powerful Is the Name of Jesus? (Acts 4:12, 24)

The name of Jesus holds **absolute power and authority** over all creation, including heaven, earth, and the underworld.

Acts 4:12 (NIV)

"Salvation is found in no one else, for there is no other name under heaven given to mankind by which we must be saved."

Acts 4:24 (NIV)

"Sovereign Lord," they said, "You made the heavens and the earth and the sea, and everything in them."

These verses emphasize:

- No other name can **save, heal, or deliver** like the name of Jesus.
- His name holds authority over **every force of darkness, sickness, and oppression**.
- Every prayer, every command, and every victory is sealed in the name of Jesus!

4. How Do I Engage the Name of Jesus in My Life?

To see the power of the name of Jesus in your life, you must **actively engage** it by:

1. **Speaking it in Faith** – Declare His name over every situation (1 Samuel 17:45).
2. **Praying in His Name** – Seal your prayers in Jesus' name (John 14:13-14).
3. **Worshipping His Name** – Exalt His name through praise (Psalm 34:3).
4. **Proclaiming it in Spiritual Warfare** – Use His name against demonic attacks (Mark 16:17).

5. **Walking in Obedience** – His name works powerfully when we live according to His Word (John 15:7).

5. The Name of Jesus and Your Health

Jesus' name carries healing power. When spoken in faith, sickness, disease, and afflictions must bow.

Acts 3:6 (NIV):

"Silver or gold I do not have, but what I do have I give you. In the name of Jesus Christ of Nazareth, walk."

- The lame man was healed instantly because of the power in Jesus' name.

- Every sickness has a name—cancer, diabetes, high blood pressure—but the name of Jesus is **above every name** (Philippians 2:9-10).

- **Declare:** *"In the name of Jesus, I receive healing in my body!"*

A mother once shared how she prayed over her child's persistent fever, declaring healing in Jesus' name, and the fever broke within hours. Such moments remind us that His name still heals today.

6. The Name of Jesus and Your Protection (Spiritual Warfare)

The name of Jesus is a **strong tower** and a weapon of warfare.

Proverbs 18:10 (NIV):

"The name of the Lord is a fortified tower; the righteous run to it and are safe."

- Demons tremble and flee at the mention of His name (Mark 16:17).
- The name of Jesus shields you from every form of spiritual opposition, including unseen forces that seek to harm or hinder your destiny (Luke 10:19).
- **Declare:** *"I cover myself and my family in the name of Jesus—no weapon formed against us shall prosper!"*

7. The Name of Jesus and Your Deliverance (Isaiah 45:1-3)

(Isaiah 45:2-3 NIV):

"I will go before you and will level the mountains; I will break down gates of bronze and cut through bars of iron. I will give you hidden treasures, riches stored in secret places."

Though originally spoken to Cyrus, this passage reflects God's promise to break barriers and lead His people into freedom—physically, emotionally, and spiritually. Through Jesus, we too experience these divine breakthroughs.

- The name of Jesus breaks chains of addiction, depression, and oppression.
- It unlocks doors of freedom and shatters the works of the enemy.

- **Declare:** *"In the name of Jesus, every chain in my life is broken!"*

7. The Name of Jesus and Your Provision Jesus' name guarantees divine provision and supernatural supply.

Philippians 4:19 (NIV):

"And my God will meet all your needs according to the riches of His glory in Christ Jesus."

- His name grants access to God's limitless resources.
- When you pray in Jesus' name, supernatural provision manifests.
- **Declare:** *"In the name of Jesus, I receive divine provision and financial breakthrough!"*

9. The Name of Jesus and Your Strength/Encouragement

When you feel weak, weary, or discouraged, His name provides supernatural strength.

Isaiah 40:29 (NIV):

"He gives strength to the weary and increases the power of the weak."

- His name renews your strength and uplifts your spirit.

- When you feel overwhelmed, call on His name, and He will restore your joy.
- Declare: *"In the name of Jesus, I receive divine strength and courage!"*

10. The Name of Jesus and Your Peace

His name brings **peace in every storm**—emotional, financial, spiritual, or physical.

John 14:27 (NIV):

"Peace I leave with you; my peace I give you. I do not give to you as the world gives. Do not let your hearts be troubled and do not be afraid."

- The name of Jesus calms anxiety, fear, and confusion.
- When troubled, **speak His name over your mind and spirit**.
- **Declare:** *"In the name of Jesus, I receive peace that surpasses understanding!"*

Now that we've explored the spiritual dimensions of Jesus' name, let's examine how this truth plays out in everyday life. The following is the story of Mark, a man whose life was radically changed by applying the principles we've just discussed.

Mark's Journey

Mark was known as someone who thrived in the corporate world, making strides in his career with commendable achievements. However, over time, he found himself struggling with stress and a crisis he couldn't quite name. Work pressures grew, and his once-stellar health began to wane. It wasn't long before Mark felt as though he was constantly battling against an invisible force, with little to no reprieve. Despite his best efforts, he often felt overwhelmed, which began to affect his relationships and mindset.

Deep down, Mark sensed that his struggle was beyond physical or mental burnout. During a conversation with a close friend, he learned about the power of spiritual warfare, particularly the potent combination of *fasting and invoking the name of Jesus*. Intrigued and in need of a breakthrough, he decided to explore this path further.

Mark embarked on a dedicated month-long spiritual regimen. He began fasting regularly, initially to detoxify his body and mind, but soon realized the deeper spiritual connection it brought. Through fasting, he focused his thoughts, cleared clutter from his heart, and sought divine strength to guide him through his struggles.

In parallel, Mark began invoking the *name of Jesus* with conviction. Each challenge he faced was met with aloud declarations of strength and patience through Christ. He would say, "In the name of Jesus, I command clarity. I command peace. I claim joy." These words became his mantra, reinforcing his faith and invoking the divine intervention he sought.

As weeks passed, something remarkable happened. The chaos that once clouded his mind began to dissipate. Work pressure became manageable, stress reduced significantly, and he found renewed vigor in approaching daily obstacles. Moreover, an unexpected contract landed on his desk—an opportunity that shifted not just his professional trajectory but also fortified his financial standing.

The change in Mark was evident to everyone around him. With renewed faith, he approached problems with a previously unrecognized strength, crediting his breakthrough to the potent use of fasting and the powerful invocation of Jesus' name. His testimony soon became a beacon of hope for many of his colleagues and friends, inspiring them to explore the spiritual dimensions of their lives.

Mark's transformation is proof that spiritual battles require spiritual strategies. By invoking the name of Jesus with faith and discipline, he didn't just survive—he triumphed. His life now inspires others to do the same.

Final Declaration: Victory in the Name of Jesus

"Father, in the name of Jesus, I declare total victory in every area of my life! I stand in the authority of His

name and break every limitation, sickness, oppression, and attack of the enemy. I receive divine healing, provision, peace, and strength. I enforce my destiny, and I walk in supernatural favor. In the mighty name of Jesus, Amen!"

Action Plan Recap

1. Declare and Affirm

Are you consistently declaring His name over your life situations? Make it a habit to pray in Jesus' name and speak His authority over your challenges (John 14:13-14). This regular invocation reinforces His power and presence in every aspect of your life.

2. Engage in Spiritual Warfare

When adversity strikes, don't just react—respond with the Word and the name of Jesus. How often do you turn to His name during battles? Utilize it as your tool in spiritual warfare, knowing it holds authority over any demonic forces (Mark 16:17).

3. Seek Healing and Provision

Do you trust in the healing and provision power inherent in Jesus' name? Declare His name over areas needing healing and provision. Remember, His name rises above every ailment and scarcity (Philippians 2:9-10). Rely on it as your anchor for divine intervention.

4. **Reinforce Your Spiritual Growth**

   How often do you incorporate Jesus' name into your spiritual practices? Use it to gain strength, encouragement, and peace. By praying in His name and meditating on scriptures, fortify your faith, making Jesus the cornerstone of your spiritual journey.

5. **Maintain Obedience**

   Is your life aligned with obedience to His Word? Ensuring you live in accordance with His teachings amplifies the power of invoking His name (John 15:7). This alignment not only strengthens your declarations but empowers you to live abundantly under His divine authority.

By integrating these steps, you can harness the transformative power encapsulated in the name of Jesus, confidently navigating life's challenges and seizing the spiritual authority He imparts. Prepare to witness change as you deepen this practice in your daily life.

CHAPTER 10

POWER OF THE WORD

The Word of God is more than just ink on pages—it's the bedrock of our faith, the essence of God's will revealed to mankind. Understanding the Word is essential because it shapes our identity, informs our choices, and reveals God's promises.

1. **What Is the Word?**

The **Word of God** is:

- **The spoken, written, and living revelation of God.**
- **God's Eternal Truth** (John 17:17).
- **Alive and Active** (Hebrews 4:12).

2. **Who Is the Word?**

- Jesus is the Word made flesh (John 1:1, 14).
- The Word is God's eternal expression and power (Matthew 24:35).
- It creates, sustains, and transforms lives (Hebrews 1:3).

3. How Powerful Is the Word?

The Word of God is a profound force that brings transformation and life to all who engage with it.

- Acts 4:12 & 24: The Word is central to salvation and transformation, offering a life-altering path to those who embrace it.
- Psalm 107:20: With its healing and deliverance, the Word acts as a powerful agent of restoration.
- Hebrews 4:12: Piercing the heart and discerning thoughts, the Word of God changes lives, providing clarity and divine insight.

    Understanding the Word's transformative power, let us explore how to actively apply it in everyday life.

4. How Do I Apply the Word in My Life?

Integrating the Word into daily life involves thoughtful engagement and active participation.

- Store It First (Psalm 119:11): Memorize and meditate on the Word, safeguarding it within your heart.
- Speak It (Joshua 1:8): Your declarations give life to the Word, influencing your circumstances with divine authority.
- Act on It (James 1:22): Live out God's commands, transforming knowledge into obedient action.

With the Word stored, spoken, and acted upon, consider its significant impact on your health. For instance: When Maria faced unemployment, she memorized Psalm 23, declared it daily, and chose to remain faithful and optimistic. Within weeks, not only did peace replace her anxiety, but doors opened for a new job she hadn't even *applied* for.

5. The Word and Your Health

The Word facilitates healing and vitality, sustaining life.

- Proverbs 4:20-22: It breathes life and health, acting as medicine for the body and soul.

- Psalm 107:20: God's sent Word restores health, defeating disease and affliction.

- Isaiah 53:5: Through Christ's atonement, His Word ensures our healing.

  Not only does the Word heal our bodies, but it also guards our spirits. Let's explore how it acts as our divine protection.

6. The Word and Your Protection (Spiritual Warfare)

In spiritual battles, the Word serves as our defense and strength.

- Ephesians 6:17: The Word is the Spirit's sword, cutting through deception and lies.

- Psalm 91:4: As a shield, it offers safety and security, reaffirming trust.

- Matthew 4:4, 7, 10: Jesus exemplified how the Word can defeat Satan, showcasing its power in spiritual warfare.

While bolstering spiritual defenses, the Word also facilitates deliverance and freedom.

7. The Word and Your Deliverance

Deliverance is assured through the power of the Word.

- John 8:32: Its truth liberates from bondage, enlightening paths to freedom.
- Luke 4:18: The Word is proclaimed to deliver those bound by oppression.

The Word not only delivers but also provides abundantly.

8. The Word and Your Provision

God's Word ensures our needs are met, providing assurance of supply.

- Philippians 4:19: His promises guarantee provision, regardless of circumstance.
- Deuteronomy 8:3: We thrive not just on physical sustenance but by every Word from God.
- Malachi 3:10: Faithful application of the Word unlocks divine financial blessings.

While meeting provision, the Word strengthens and encourages us for life's journey. His Word assures us that God knows our needs—both material and spiritual. Whether it's peace in a storm or food on the table, the Word reminds us that our Provider is faithful.

9. The Word and Your Strength/Encouragement

Strength and encouragement are found in the promises of the Word.

- Isaiah 40:31: Renews and invigorates, ensuring you soar amidst challenges.
- Joshua 1:9: Encourages courage and confidence, equipping you to face trials.
- Psalm 119:28: Uplifts and strengthens in times of distress.

Beyond temporal strength, the Word brings peace that surpasses understanding.

10. The Word and Your Peace

The Word is a wellspring of peace, calming hearts and minds.

- John 14:27: Offers profound peace, setting aside worldly turmoil.
- Philippians 4:7: Guards hearts with peace that transcends comprehension.
- Isaiah 26:3: Keeping our minds on His Word assures perfect peace.

With these insights, the significant role of the Word in guiding, protecting, and nurturing every aspect of our lives comes into clearer focus. Each segment reveals a depth of purpose, urging believers to engage and rely upon the Word in diverse circumstances, yielding its transformative power.

DECLARATION: WALKING IN SUPERNATURAL VICTORY

"Father, in the name of Jesus, I receive the full power of Your name, the Holy Spirit, and the Word of God. I stand in divine authority over every sickness, lack, fear, and oppression. I declare health, provision, strength, and peace over my life. Holy Spirit, guide me, empower me, and protect me. Let Your Word be a lamp unto my feet and a light unto my path. I walk in supernatural victory, in Jesus' mighty name! Amen!"

Speak this declaration aloud with faith—or even write your own based on the Scriptures that spoke to you in this chapter.

Action Plan Recap

- Engage with the Word Actively

    As you walk with God daily, let His Word guide you. Keep it close to your heart through memorization and meditation, allowing it to be your ever-present guide (Psalm 119:11). This daily engagement ensures that the Word remains a cornerstone in your life decisions.

- Proclaim and Act on the Word

Do you regularly declare the Word over your life situations? Make it a habit to speak His promises boldly and live by its teachings. When you actively declare and act on the Word (Joshua 1:8; James 1:22), you unleash its transforming power into your circumstances.

- Harness the Word for Health and Protection

When facing trials, do you rely on the Word as your source of healing and defense? Trust the Word to be your healing balm and protective shield in spiritual battles (Proverbs 4:20-22; Ephesians 6:17). Let it be your primary source for both physical wellness and spiritual safeguarding.

- Use the Word for Provision and Strength

Are you leaning on the Word to meet your needs and bolster your inner strength? Apply its teachings to unlock God's provision and reinforce your resilience (Philippians 4:19; Isaiah 40:31). The Word not only supplies your needs but also sustains you through life's ups and downs.

- Live in Peace through the Word

Do you focus your mind on the peace promised by God's Word? By allowing His Word to guide your thoughts and actions, you can endure challenging times with tranquility (John 14:27; Isaiah 26:3). Let His promises usher in a peace that surpasses all understanding, guarding your heart in every season of life.

With every step, your engagement with the Word brings its full spectrum of healing, strength, peace, and provision into your life, empowering you to live more fully in its light.

CHAPTER 11

ACTIVATING YOUR SPIRITUAL WEAPONS

Be Born Again

To effectively engage these weapons, you must first surrender your life to Jesus Christ as your Lord and Savior.

Understanding the Path to Being Born Again: The Roman Road to Salvation

Introduction: The Journey to New Life

Being born again means starting a new life through faith in Jesus Christ. It's more than just a single moment; it's the beginning of a renewed relationship with God. This spiritual rebirth is guided by grace, and the Roman Road to Salvation helps us understand how to take each step along the way.

Big Idea

The journey to being born again is a step-by-step path of recognizing our sin, accepting Jesus Christ as Savior, and confessing our faith aloud. This transformation is clearly mapped out in Scripture through what is known as the Roman Road to Salvation.

Understanding Our Need for Salvation

The journey to salvation begins with acknowledging our universal need. Romans 3:23 speaks candidly, reminding us, "All have sinned and fall short of the glory of God." This understanding is pivotal as it sheds light on our human limitations and the gap between us and a holy God. Such recognition nurtures humility and inspires an earnest search for divine grace.

Having acknowledged our need for salvation, we are then led to the most hopeful truth—the gift of eternal life, freely offered through Jesus Christ.

Embracing God's Gift

While the weight of sin carries significant consequences, Romans 6:23 offers a transformational promise: "For the wages of sin is death, but the gift of God is eternal life in Christ Jesus our Lord." This scripture highlights the dichotomy between sin's consequence and God's generous gift of salvation. It invites us to understand that eternal life is not an earned reward but a gracious gift, providing hope and the assurance of redemption.

Once we embrace this divine gift, our response turns toward confession and belief, the critical steps in our faith journey.

The Act of Confession and Belief

Romans 10:9-10 captures the critical actions of declaring, "Jesus is Lord," and believing in the resurrection. These verses underscore the dual essence of faith—public confession and sincere belief. Through both, believers make a commitment not just in their hearts but through their words, marking the beginning of a transformed life.

This step of confession ushers in a transformation, leading us to live a renewed life filled with growth and purpose.

The Wrap-Up — Living the New Life

Embarking on this path to being born again offers an invitation to a life of transformation, continually nurtured by faith, empowered by grace, and defined by an enduring relationship with God. The Roman Road to Salvation is more than a passage from sin to redemption; it's the foundation for ongoing spiritual growth and connection to divine purpose. It beckons believers to embrace spiritual rebirth—a perpetual horizon of growth and fulfillment, illuminated by each step of faith.

These transitional sentences articulate the progression from recognizing our spiritual need to embracing the gift and committing to a life of faith, creating a seamless and contemplative journey through the Roman Road to Salvation.

Just as a caterpillar becomes a butterfly, life after spiritual rebirth brings visible change—new desires, deeper peace, and a drive to walk in love and truth each day.

The Romans Road to Salvation

- All have sinned and fall short of the glory of God (Romans 3:23).
- The wages of sin is death (Romans 6:23).
- The free gift of God is eternal life in Christ Jesus our Lord (Romans 6:23b).
- Confess with your mouth that Jesus is Lord and believe in your heart that God raised Him from the dead (Romans 10:9-10).

A Simple Prayer for Salvation

Confession of Belief in Jesus

Jesus, I believe with all my heart that you are the Son of God, that you died on the cross to rescue me from sin and death and to restore me to the Father (Romans 10:9-10).

Turning from Sin

I choose now to turn from my sins, my self-centeredness, and every part of my life that does not please you. I choose you, Jesus. I give myself to you, Jesus (1 John 1:9).

Asking for the Holy Spirit

I receive your forgiveness and ask you to take your rightful place in my life as my Savior and Lord. I ask in the name of Jesus that I receive the gift of the Holy Spirit, which will lead me into all truth. May I now be filled with the Holy Spirit (Luke 11:13).

Declaration of Identity

Jesus, come reign in my heart, fill me with your love and your life, and help me to become a person who is truly loving—a person like you, Jesus. Restore me, Jesus. Live in me. Love through me. I declare and decree that I am no longer a slave; I am a child of God. I am chosen and not forsaken. God hasn't given me a spirit of fear, but of power, love, and a sound mind (2 Corinthians 5:17, 2 Timothy 1:7).

Thanksgiving and Amen

Thank you, God. In Jesus' name, I pray. Amen (1 Thessalonians 5:18, John 14:13-14).

Action Plan Recap

1. Accept Salvation and Declare Your Faith

Acknowledge your need for Jesus, receive His gift of eternal life, and boldly confess your belief (Romans 10:9). Let this be the cornerstone of your spiritual empowerment.

2. Commit with Prayer

Engage in a heartfelt prayer to invite Jesus as your Lord and Savior. This marks the beginning of your transformative journey and spiritual rebirth (Revelation 3:20).

3. Invite the Holy Spirit

Ask the Holy Spirit to fill your life, guiding you to truth and empowering you with divine strength. This is pivotal for wielding spiritual tools effectively (John 16:13).

4. Live by the Spirit

Let your rebirth inspire you to live faithfully. Walk in Christ's teachings and allow the Holy Spirit to guide your daily choices (Galatians 5:16).

5. Declare Your Freedom and Identity

Continually affirm your identity in Christ as a reborn child of God. Embrace a life filled with power, love, and a sound mind (2 Timothy 1:7).

By consistently integrating these steps, you open yourself to transformative growth, embracing the full power and authority of spiritual life in Christ.

CHAPTER 12

USING YOUR WEAPONS

Thanksgiving (Philemon 1:6)

- Thanksgiving is a powerful spiritual weapon that activates God's presence and power in our lives. Philemon 1:6 states, "That the communication of thy faith may become effectual by the acknowledging of every good thing which is in you in Christ Jesus." In other words, when we acknowledge and give thanks for the good things God has already placed within us, our faith becomes more effective and impactful.

- **Thanksgiving magnifies God** – When we give thanks, we shift our focus from our problems to God's greatness (Psalm 100:4).

- **Thanksgiving strengthens faith** – Gratitude reminds us of God's past faithfulness, reinforcing our trust in Him (1 Thessalonians 5:18).

- **Thanksgiving invokes divine intervention** – Jesus gave thanks before multiplying the loaves and fishes (John 6:11), demonstrating that gratitude precedes breakthroughs. In spiritual warfare, this teaches us that when we thank God in faith—even before the outcome—we create an atmosphere for miracles and divine action.

- **How to Apply Thanksgiving in Spiritual Warfare:**

    1. Start prayers with gratitude for victories already won (Psalm 107:15-16).

    2. Thank God for His promises before seeing their manifestation (Psalm 103:1-5).

    3. Praise God in advance for breakthroughs (Acts 16:25-26).

Just as thanksgiving unlocks divine favor, obedience aligns us with God's power and protection.

Obedience

Obedience to God is key to activating spiritual authority and protection. Disobedience weakens our spiritual defense, while obedience keeps us aligned with God's will and power.

- **Obedience attracts divine presence** – God is close to those who obey Him (John 14:23).

- **Obedience secures divine blessings** – "If you are willing and obedient, you shall eat the good of the land" (Isaiah 1:19).

- **Obedience repels the enemy** – When we submit to God, the devil flees (James 4:7).

How to Apply Obedience in Spiritual Warfare:

1. Follow God's Word and instructions fully.
2. Repent quickly when convicted of disobedience.
3. Remain sensitive to the Holy Spirit's leading in all actions.

Alongside thanksgiving and obedience, the words we speak become powerful tools in the spiritual realm.

Your Tongue

The tongue is a spiritual weapon that can bring either life or destruction. Proverbs 18:21 says, "Death and life are in the power of the tongue." The tongue is described in James 3:6 as a fire—a world of iniquity—capable of setting the course of life on fire, highlighting its tremendous spiritual power.

- **Speaking God's Word enforces victory** – Jesus defeated Satan in the wilderness by declaring scripture (Matthew 4:4-10).

- **Declarations create spiritual realities** – What we confess aligns our circumstances with God's will (Job 22:28).

- **Praise and worship confuse the enemy** – Declaring God's greatness paralyzes the opposition (2 Chronicles 20:22).

How to Apply Your Tongue in Spiritual Warfare:

1. Speak life and not negativity over situations.

2. Declare scriptures aligned with God's promises.
3. Engage in consistent praise and prophetic declarations, which not only strengthen your spirit but also create confusion in the enemy's camp, halting their operations and enforcing heaven's agenda over your life.

Action Plan Recap

- **Integrate Thanksgiving into Daily Practice**

Begin each day with gratitude. Recognize God's past blessings and open each prayer with thanksgiving to invite His presence and reinforce your faith (Philemon 1:6, Psalm 100:4, Ephesians 5:20).

- **Commit to Obedience**

Follow God's commandments diligently. Obedience attracts His presence and secures His blessings. Stay sensitive to His leading and repent quickly when needed (John 14:23, James 4:7, Deuteronomy 28:1-2).

- **Harness the Power of Your Tongue**

Speak life over every situation. Declare God's promises and engage in regular praise. Your words create realities and can trigger divine interventions (Proverbs 18:21, Matthew 4:4-10, Job 22:28).

By consistently practicing these steps, you can harness the spiritual power available to you, ensuring a proactive and fortified spiritual journey.

CHAPTER 13

POWER OF FAITH

Faith is the shield that extinguishes all the fiery darts of the enemy (Ephesians 6:16). Without faith, it is impossible to please God (Hebrews 11:6).

- **Faith grants access to God's power** – Jesus often said, "Your faith has made you whole" (Mark 5:34).
- **Faith turns obstacles into testimonies** – Mountains move by faith-filled declarations (Mark 11:23).
- **Faith activates angelic intervention** – Angels respond to words of faith (Psalm 103:20).

How to Apply Faith in Spiritual Warfare:

1. Believe in God's promises despite circumstances.
2. Speak and act in agreement with your faith.
3. Avoid fear and doubt, replacing them with trust in God.

By using these spiritual weapons—Thanksgiving, Obedience, Your Tongue, and Your Faith—you can engage effectively in spiritual warfare and walk in victory.

Your Faith

First, understand this: faith in the Bible is a deeply personal matter. It is according to your faith that you are saved, healed, joyful, prospered, and able to receive anything God has promised—when you take the corresponding actions and meet His conditions (Matthew 9:29, Mark 9:23, Luke 17:19).

Hebrews 11:6 also tells us that without faith, we cannot please God.

Faith can be described as one of the currencies of heaven that we use to transact business and acquire heavenly blessings of all types, such as love, joy, peace, good relationships, provision, health, money, and whatever God has promised in His Word.

"Faith is the very essence of Christianity, and the Word of God is the source and foundation of faith. If this is the case—and it is—the more time you invest in the Word—reading, hearing, studying, etc.—the greater your capacity for faith will be. Notice I say capacity. The reason for this distinction is that there are four fundamental truths you must know, understand, and apply consistently for your faith to grow and develop in a way that pleases God. We will discuss these truths next. For now, let us see how essential faith is to our Christian lifestyle.

- **We Are Saved by Faith (Ephesians 2:8):** Through faith, we receive the grace of salvation, underscoring that it is not by our works but by God's gift.

- **We Live by Faith (Habakkuk 2:4; Romans 1:17; Galatians 3:11; Hebrews 10:38):** Faith is not a one-time event; it is a way of life that sustains and guides us daily on our spiritual journey.

- **We Walk by Faith (2 Corinthians 5:7):** Our faith requires us to trust in what we cannot see, leading us forward with confidence in God's promises.

- **We Stand by Faith (Romans 5:2):** In faith, we access the grace in which we stand firm, providing strength and resilience in life's challenges.

- **We Are Healed by Faith (Mark 5:34):** Faith in Jesus' power brings about physical and emotional healing, restoring wholeness.

- **We Overcome by Faith (1 John 5:4):** Our victory over the world is secured through faith, enabling us to conquer trials and tribulations.

- **We Are Called to Fight the Good Fight of Faith (1 Timothy 6:12):** Faith is an active pursuit, a lifelong battle that requires courage and perseverance.

- **We Do All Kinds of Exploits by Faith (Hebrews 11:33-34):** By faith, we achieve great things, as demonstrated by heroes in Scripture who subdued kingdoms and achieved righteousness.

These affirmations remind us that faith permeates every aspect of our spiritual lives, anchoring us in the reality of God's promises and empowering us to live victoriously.

The Four Fundamentals of Faith

Faith Is Based on the Word of God

For example, Abraham believed God's promise before he saw the fulfillment—his faith rested entirely on God's Word. This illustrates how faith is anchored not in visible reality but in the divine assurance found in Scripture (Romans 10:8).

Faith Comes by Hearing

Consider how the Israelites heard the message of deliverance and responded, knowing it was God's promise to them. This demonstrates that our faith is sparked and strengthened by continuous engagement with God's Word (Romans 10:17).

Faith Is Released by Speaking

When David faced Goliath, he declared victory in the name of the Lord before the battle began. This example highlights how spoken words of faith activate God's power and promises in our lives (Matthew 17:20, Mark 11:23).

Faith Requires Corresponding Action to Produce Results

As when Peter stepped onto the water, faith required him to get out of the boat despite the storm.

This action-oriented faith shows that belief must be coupled with action to realize God's promises (James 2:16-17).

These examples collectively showcase that faith, rooted in God's Word, heard with belief, declared with conviction, and acted upon, leads to transformative outcomes in the believer's journey.

Remember, these are the same steps you took to get saved. You heard the message, opened your mouth, confessed your sins, and invited Jesus into your life by speaking—and you were saved. That's how it works to receive every other thing from God (Romans 10:9-10).

"Let's reinforce these four fundamentals by walking through a few powerful biblical examples. Remember: the pattern remains the same—hear the Word, believe it, speak it, and act on it.

CHAPTER 14

GROWING YOUR FAITH

To develop or grow your faith, you must first know where you stand. In 2 Corinthians 13:5, the Bible encourages us to examine ourselves. This chapter will walk you through the different levels of faith outlined in Scripture, help you identify where you are, and give you tools—spiritual, practical, and personal—to begin growing your faith intentionally.

Levels of Faith

The Measure of Faith

For every believer, a measure of faith is given as a starting point, pivotal for spiritual growth (Romans 12:3, Ephesians 4:7, 1 Peter 4:10). It's not about how much faith you have initially, but how you cultivate and use it that determines your spiritual outcome. *Now that we've explored the measure of faith, let's examine what it means to have Dead Faith.*

Dead Faith

James 2:17 highlights faith without action as dead—alive in potential but dormant in action. It's the kind of faith where understanding and belief exist without commitment to follow through. Such faith offers no transformative power or results until acted upon. *Moving from dormant to active, we next consider Little Faith.*

Little Faith

Described in *Matthew* 6:30, Little Faith is easily swayed by life's trivial worries. This type of faith, while genuine, often succumbs to doubt and fear when faced with life's minor challenges. Consider the disciples during the storm on the sea, who, despite being with Jesus, were filled with fear and doubt. This illustrates how Little Faith can be shaken by everyday concerns. *With growth in mind, let's explore what it means to possess Weak Faith.*

Weak Faith

Romans 4:19 shows how Weak Faith is hindered by skepticism, often shackled by circumstances rather than freed by divine assurance. This is like Sarah in *Genesis* 18, who laughed at God's promise because her circumstances felt impossible. You may have faith, but it's constantly interrupted by "what ifs" and "yeah buts." This type of faith requires stronger roots in hope and divine certainty. *Building on understanding, let's shift our focus to Shipwreck Faith.*

Shipwreck Faith

A heart with Shipwreck Faith, as noted in *1 Timothy 1:18-20*, starts with good intentions but falters by abandoning truth. It's faith derailed by focusing on worldly distractions rather than maintaining steadfastness in spiritual goals. For example, Demas, mentioned by Paul, had faith that started strong but was shipwrecked by his love for the present world. *From setbacks, let's elevate to Great Faith.*

Great Faith

Matthew 8:10 portrays Great Faith as unwavering trust in God's word alone, unshaken by external situations. It stands firm in the understanding and assurance of God's promises, leading to miraculous outcomes. *Evolving further, let's look at Strong Faith.*

Strong Faith

Romans 4:20 characterizes Strong Faith by its resilience, asking confidently, "Is God able?" and affirming His capabilities without doubt. It's faith that praises God amidst trial, knowing His word is true. It's Great Faith plus Praising God. *Beyond strength, we reach Genuine Faith.*

Genuine Faith

Emphasized in 2 Timothy 1:5, Genuine Faith is generational and sincere, rooted in the teachings passed from loved ones. It remains true to the Word regardless of challenges, deeply affecting one's spiritual lineage. *Continuing growth leads us to examine Growing Faith.*

Growing/Ever-Increasing Faith

2 Thessalonians 1:3 depicts Growing Faith as intentional and dynamic, expanding through ongoing practice of the Word—hearing, speaking, and acting. It's the faith that continuously evolves through dedication. *From growth to stability, we see the fortitude of Unwavering Faith.*

Unwavering Faith

Hebrews 10:23 celebrates Unwavering Faith for its steadfastness in God's promises, remaining unaffected by sensory experiences. This faith focuses entirely on praise and thanksgiving, standing firm in the assurance of fulfillment. *Thank you, Jesus, for such profound faith!*

This exploration of faith levels clarifies stages of spiritual development and encourages continuous growth and actionable trust in God's promises.

Now that we have the list, where do you stand?

Levels of Faith Chart

Level of Faith	Description	Scriptural Support
Dead Faith	Faith without results due to a lack of action. Engages in religious activities but lacks intentional spiritual growth. Can be revived by the Word.	James 2:17, Romans 2:13, Titus 3:8

Little Faith	Suffers from doubt and worry despite hearing the Word. Capitulates to life's small issues and anxieties, often fixating on fears of the future.	Matthew 6:30, Matthew 8:26, Matthew 16:8
Weak Faith	Easily swayed by circumstances, with doubts and frequent 'yea but' scenarios. Tends to focus more on challenges than possibilities.	Romans 4:19, Luke 1:18, Genesis 15:5-6
Shipwreck Faith	Begins in the right direction but falters, driven by a corrupted conscience and worldly distractions.	1 Timothy 1:18-20, 2 Timothy 2:18, Revelation 3:1
Great Faith	Possesses a strong understanding of God's faith principles and His Word. Knows that God's angels uphold His promises, leading to confident requests and expectations.	Matthew 8:10, John 4:50-53, Matthew 15:28
Strong Faith	Resolute and unfazed by circumstances, asking only if God can perform His promises, bolstered by belief and giving glory to God.	Romans 4:20, Luke 1:45, 2 Corinthians 5:7
Genuine Faith	A transgenerational belief nurtured by Word-based principles passed down through family.	2 Timothy 1:5, 2 Timothy 3:14-15, 1 John 5:4

	Acknowledges how personal faith impacts future generations.	
Growing Faith	Applies the fundamentals of faith (Word, Hearing, Speaking, Action) consistently, building steadily over weeks; encouraged by the 50/10 formula (50 minutes reading, 10 minutes aloud).	2 Thessalonians 1:3, 2 Peter 1:5-8, Acts 16:5
Unwavering Faith	A fully persuaded belief not swayed by what is seen or heard, but anchored in the Word. Focuses entirely on praise and thanksgiving after prayer until results manifest.	Hebrews 10:23, Hebrews 4:14, 1 Thessalonians 5:24

This chart provides a clear visualization of different faith levels, their characteristics, and corresponding scriptures to help believers pinpoint where they currently stand and how to progress spiritually.

Take a moment. Ask yourself: Where is my faith today? What would it take for me to move to the next level? What specific steps will I commit to this week to grow my faith?

Faith Level Tracker with Meditations and Prayers

Purpose:

"Use this worksheet as a daily companion to your spiritual routine. Whether you're journaling in the morning or reflecting at night, it will help you stay accountable, track your growth, and apply what you're learning about faith. Print it out or keep a digital version for daily check-ins.

This worksheet is intended to help you monitor and nurture your spiritual growth, specifically focusing on the development of your faith. Use the meditations and prayers associated with each level of faith to guide your inner reflection and strengthen your spiritual journey.

Personal Information:

- **Name:**
- **Date:**

Faith Evaluation Metrics:

1. **Daily Engagement with the Word of God:**
   - Frequency: Daily / Weekly / Occasionally / Rarely
   - Notes and Reflections:

2. **Hearing and Meditation:**
   - Time Spent (e.g., listening to audio sermons, participating in discussions):
   - Key Insights Obtained:

3. **Speaking and Declarations:**
   - How Often Do You Make Faith Declarations?
   - Examples of Declarations Used:

4. **Corresponding Actions Taken:**
   - Describe Actions Taken in Faith (e.g., acts of kindness, service):
   - Results or Outcomes Observed:

Faith Levels with Meditations and Prayers:

- **Dead Faith:**
  - **Prayer:** "Lord, breathe life into my faith. Guide me to actions that reflect belief and trust in You. Awaken my spirit to Your call and lead me to live out my faith with purpose."

- **Little Faith:**
  - **Meditation:** "Reflect on God's past faithfulness. Remember times when even small acts of faith produced great outcomes, knowing that He never fails."

Prayer: "Heavenly Father, strengthen my faith. Help me overcome doubt and worry, trusting Your word over my fears."

- **Weak Faith:**
  - **Meditation:** "Consider the growth potential within every doubt—a place where God's power is perfected in weakness."
  - **Prayer:** "Help me, Lord, to trust Your promises above my circumstances. Strengthen my belief and fortify my faith against challenges."
- **Strong Faith:**
  - **Meditation:** "Envision the unwavering confidence in God's promises. Reflect on moments of spiritual victories achieved through faith."
  - **Prayer:** "Father, embolden my faith to speak and act with certainty. Grant me the strength to stand firm and relentless in my trust."
- **Genuine Faith:**
  - **Meditation:** "Explore the legacy of faith you create, envisioning the impact of a deeply rooted, unwavering belief."
  - **Prayer:** "Lord, may my faith be genuine and pure, a reflection of my love for You. Let it be a beacon to others, drawing them closer to Your presence."
- **Growing/Ever Increasing Faith:**

- **Meditation:** "Visualize your faith expanding daily, fueled by the Word and deeds. Acknowledge this growth as a journey, not a destination."
- **Prayer:** "Thank You, Lord, for the opportunity to grow my faith. May I continually seek Your truth, acting boldly in alignment with Your Word."

- **Unwavering Faith:**
  - **Meditation:** "Pause in gratitude for the stability and peace that unwavering faith brings, an anchor amidst life's tempests."
  - **Prayer:** "Heavenly Father, thank You for the strength to weather life's storms. I rest in Your promises, assured and steadfast in Your love."

Reflection and Goal Setting:

- **Current Focus Areas:** (e.g., Consistency, Specific Promises)
- **Short-term Goals (Next 30 Days):**
- **Long-term Goals (6 Months):**
- **Action Steps to Achieve Goals:**

Use these reflections and prayers regularly to assess and enhance your faith journey, adapting as you grow and deepen your spiritual practice.

Specific Action Steps to Start Growing Your Faith Right Now

Here is the good news: to start growing your faith right now, begin with these steps:

1. Faith Is Based on The Word.

Engage with the Word and participate in Word-based study. You are doing that now, so congratulate yourself; you're already on your way.

2. Faith Comes by Hearing.

Remember, faith comes by hearing (Romans 10:8, 17). Ideally, invest at least one hour daily in pure Bible reading. You can do this while listening to the audio version on your phone. We will provide more suggestions for your Bible reading plan later.

3. Faith Is Released by Speaking.

Faith is released by speaking (Luke 17:5-6, Matthew 17:20, 2 Corinthians 4:13). Practice the 50/10 Power Formula: read or hear the Word for 50 minutes, then read aloud for 10 minutes or more. Better yet, make a list of scriptures you want to memorize (Proverbs 7:1-3) and read them out loud for 10 minutes daily. You can use some of the declarations and prayers in this guide or create your own.

Additionally, select portions of scripture to read aloud daily until they become a part of you, such as Psalms 19, 20, 23, 27, 35, 90, 91, 92, 100, 103, 107, 119,

121, etc., as well as Proverbs 3, 4, 5, 6, 7, and 8, Ephesians 6:10–19, Hebrews chapter 11, and Revelation chapters 1, 5, and 12 for starters.

4. Take Corresponding Action.

If you desire spiritual power, spend time in the Word and pray. Become a consistent member of a Prayer/Bible Study Group. If you don't have one, join us on Tuesdays from 8:00 PM to 10:00 PM EST on Facebook Live or YouTube.

If Your Need is for Health:

- **Serve the Lord (Exodus 23:25-26):** Serving brings His blessings and health.
- **Dedicate 10% of Your Weekly Time to Service:** Commit this time weekly for the next 90 days.
- **Join a Prayer Group or Start One:** Prayer is a powerful service to the Lord (Luke 2:37).
- **Evaluate the Impact after 90 Days:** Reflect on improvements in health and life.

If Your Need is Finances:

- **Start Giving of Your Finances:** Pay your tithes and offerings to unlock blessings.
- **Embrace the Principle of Giving:** "Give, and it will be given to you" reflects this promise.
- **Trust in Divine Provision:** God's principles assure financial provision when followed (Malachi 3:10).

If Your Need is a Supportive Community:

- **Prioritize Church Attendance:** Regular fellowship provides spiritual support.
- **Get Involved Actively:** Participate in groups or activities that enhance community bonds.
- **Choose Engagement Over Excuses:** Embrace the strength that comes from connection and accountability.

If Your Need is Better Relationships:

- Practice Being a Friend to Have Friends: Kindness and patience are key.
- Follow the Second Commandment: Reflect deeply on 1 Corinthians 13 and Colossians 3:8-25.
- Cultivate Empathy and Understanding: Let these qualities guide you in building stronger bonds.

If It's a Marital Issue:

- **Focus on Love and Respect:** Explore guidance in Ephesians 5:18-33 for marital harmony.
- **Prioritize Communication and Compassion:** Key components in nurturing relationships.
- **Seek Mutual Understanding:** Work towards resolving differences and fostering unity.

If You Have Issues with Parents or Children:

- **Refer to Ephesians 6:1-4:** Use scripture to guide familial relationships.

- **Promote a Culture of Respect and Love:** Establish these values at home.
- **Encourage Open Communication:** Strengthen and support family connections.

If Your Issue is Work Related:

- **Study Ephesians 6:5-9:** Let this guide your work ethics and relationships.
- **Commit to Excellence and Integrity:** Essential for professional growth.
- **Seek to Serve as Serving Christ:** Transform workplace challenges by reframing your perspective.

Approach each challenge with faith and proactive steps, guided by scriptural wisdom, to bring profound transformation and growth.

Make these declarations, which can also serve as prayer points: *"I am a child of God, born of the Spirit of God, filled with the Spirit of God, and led by the Spirit of God. I have great, strong, and unwavering faith, and by the grace of God, I am an action taker. I am taking corresponding action consistently, in the Name of Jesus."* John 1:12, Mark 11:22-24, Matthew 17:20

"I have great faith because I take God at His word and I am taking consistent corresponding action." Matthew 8:10, James 2:16-17, Job 22:28

"I have strong faith and I am giving glory to God, thanking Him and praising Him because I am fully

persuaded that God is able to perform what He has promised." Romans 4:20, 1 Thessalonians 5:18, Hebrews 10:36

"I have unwavering faith. I am holding fast to my confession of faith in God's promises; I boldly confess what God has said in the Name of Jesus, and it is so in my life; I have what I say." Hebrews 10:23, Hebrews 13:5-6, Mark 11:23

By using these spiritual weapons—Thanksgiving, Obedience, Your Tongue, and Your Faith—you can engage effectively in spiritual warfare and walk in victory.

Faith Development Journal: 30-Day Growth Plan from Little Faith to Strong Faith

Day 1: Self-Assessment and Goal Setting

- **Reflect:** Where do you currently see your faith? (E.g., little, wavering, growing)
- **Journal:** Write down your current feelings and thoughts about your faith journey.
- **Set Goals:** Define what "strong faith" looks like for you.

Days 2-10: Building Foundations

- **Word Engagement:** Spend time daily reading and meditating on scriptures that speak about faith. Record insights and revelations.
- **Journal:** At the end of each day, note how engaging with the Word has impacted your day.

Days 11-15: Speaking and Declaring Faith

- **Practice Speaking:** Choose a set of faith declarations to say out loud each day.
- **Journal:** Record changes in your mindset or circumstances as a result of these declarations.

Days 16-20: Taking Corresponding Actions

- **Act on Faith:** Identify areas where you can take a step of faith. Whether small or big, take at least one faith-driven action each day.
- **Journal:** Reflect on the outcomes and how acting on faith has influenced your trust in God.

Days 21-25: Overcoming Doubt and Fear

- **Mental Shift:** Focus on combating doubt and fear with prayer and positive affirmations.
- **Journal:** Document any moments of challenge or victory and how you overcame negative emotions with faith.

Days 26-30: Evaluating Growth and Planning Ahead

- **Self-Evaluation:** Reflect on Day 1's entry. Compare where you started to where you are now.
- **Journal:** Celebrate the victories, acknowledge the struggles, and write a new faith goal for the next month.

Action Plan Recap

- **Deepen Engagement with the Word:** Invest consistent time in reading and meditating on the

Word of God. This strengthens your understanding and expands your faith, as faith comes from hearing the Word (Romans 10:17). Aim for a structured Bible study routine, perhaps using the suggested 50/10 power formula—50 minutes of reading and 10 minutes of speaking the Word aloud.

- **Activate Faith through Speaking and Action:** Beyond mere belief, express your faith by speaking declarations and taking corresponding actions aligned with God's promises. Release your faith by verbalizing scripture-backed affirmations and tackling actions that reflect your trust in God's power and provision.

- **Assess and Grow in Faith:** Regularly evaluate where you stand in your faith journey by identifying which level of faith you currently possess, whether it's weak, growing, or strong. Use this assessment to develop a personalized plan for growth, focusing on transitioning from dead or little faith to great and unwavering faith.

- **Embrace Faith as a Full Lifestyle:** Incorporate faith into every aspect of your life, recognizing it as fundamental to salvation, health, and overcoming challenges. Utilize faith to propel you through adversities, ensuring you remain steadfast in your values and approach situations with a perspective of victory.

- **Leverage Faith for Personal and Communal Impact:** Use your strengthened faith not only for personal development but also to influence and inspire those around you. Encourage and uplift others by testifying to the transformative power of faith and by actively engaging in communal faith-building activities like church services and prayer groups.

By systematically implementing these steps, you can cultivate a robust faith that significantly enhances your spiritual journey and enables you to walk in victory.

CHAPTER 15

FAITH THROUGH DELAYS

Delays: Divine Timing, Not Denials

In the spiritual journey, *delays* often stretch our patience and test our faith. Yet, scripturally, delays are not indicative of denial but rather of God's perfect timing. *Habakkuk 2:3* reassures us that even if the vision seems slow to arrive, "it will surely come; it will not delay." These delays serve as periods of divine preparation, allowing God to align circumstances and strengthen us for the promises He has in store.

Unveiling the Purpose of Delays

Caleb's Perseverance: Caleb exemplifies steadfast faith in the face of prolonged delays. After scouting Canaan, he returned with a positive report and urged the Israelites to seize the land (Numbers 13:30). Despite his faith, he waited over 40 years to claim his inheritance (Joshua 14:10-11). Caleb's unwavering faith, even in his advanced years, highlights the strength and reward of patient endurance grounded in trust and vision.

Zacharias and Elizabeth: The story of Zacharias and Elizabeth, parents of John the Baptist, serves as a profound testament to faith through waiting. Despite their devoutness and prayers for a child, their plea seemed unanswered until divine timing unfolded (Luke 1:13). Zacharias' temporary muteness symbolizes the reflective silence and deepened faith that can accompany divine delay, culminating in joyous prophecy and praise at John's birth (Luke 1:64-79).

Active Waiting: Living in Faithful Assurance

To wait *actively* means to engage fully with life, harnessing faith through prayer, worship, and scripture study, as suggested in *James 5:7-8*. Much like a farmer tending to the soil, believers sow seeds of faith, trust, and service during these waiting periods, maintaining spiritual readiness.

Prayers and Reflections During Delay

Prayer serves as both a lifeline and an anchor. A sample prayer during times of delay might be:

"Father, in the name of Jesus, teach me to trust in Your timing, to find strength in waiting, and to embrace each day as a gift. Renew my spirit with peace and patience as I stand on Your promises, knowing that You are faithful to fulfill them. Amen."

"Lord, as I wait, teach me to walk with You daily—not in anxiety, but in expectancy. Let worship be my strength, obedience my offering, and discernment my compass. Show me the divine in the daily and anchor my hope in Your unchanging Word. In Jesus's name, I pray. Amen."

Concluding Thoughts: Waiting as a Spiritual Discipline

Embracing waiting periods with faith transforms delays into opportunities for growth. Delays refine our character and enhance our readiness for eventual blessings, clarifying our vision and purpose within God's kingdom. As believers, maintaining active engagement, persistent faith, and consistent prayer prepares us for the fulfillment of God's promises in His perfect timing, ensuring that each delay deepens our spiritual resilience and enriches our spiritual journey.

While we wait on God's perfect timing, we are not left defenseless. The waiting season is also a spiritual battleground—one where faith must be active, not idle. During these times, believers are called to wield their spiritual weapons, not to force God's hand but to stand firm, empowered and alert. The following testimonies showcase how these divine tools sustain, protect, and propel us even as we wait.

Empowered Waiting: Real-Life Stories of Faith in Action

Unleashing Spiritual Weapons in Everyday Life

The battle for spiritual wellness often revolves around invoking divine power through faith, and everyday believers have access to an arsenal of spiritual weapons designed to empower us during challenges. Each testimony herein highlights the transformative impact of employing *Angels, The Blood of Jesus, The Holy Spirit, The Name of Jesus,* and *The Word of God* in real-life situations.

A Turnaround Through Angelic Intervention

Before experiencing a breakthrough, Mary, a devoted mother of three, faced a severe financial crisis after unexpectedly losing her job. Having always been employed since her twenties, this sudden shift left her feeling unsteady and unsure of her future. In her distress, Mary turned to her faith for support and guidance. She discovered Hebrews 1:14, realizing that angels are ministering spirits sent to serve those who will inherit salvation. With renewed hope, she committed her concerns to prayer each night, asking God to deploy His angels for her protection and provision. Miraculously, opportunities began to emerge, starting with a job offer that seemed to come out of nowhere. Her story demonstrates the unwavering faith that empowers believers to activate angelic support in times of desperation.

The Protective Power of The Blood of Jesus

John, a seasoned travel nurse, often encountered intense pressure from high-stakes situations and unforeseen medical emergencies. During a particularly overwhelming healthcare crisis, he found himself on the front lines, feeling both anxious and determined. Reminded of the power in The Blood of Jesus, John began each day by pleading for divine protection, invoking Revelation 12:11: "They triumphed over him by the blood of the Lamb and by the word of their testimony." To his amazement, peace replaced his anxiety, and he witnessed a calming transformation in his work environment, attributing this newfound tranquility to the protective invocation of the blood.

Guidance from The Holy Spirit

Samantha, a recent university graduate, was mired in uncertainty about her career path. With several job offers and potential city relocations on the horizon, she felt overwhelmed by decision-making pressures. Seeking clarity, Samantha leaned into her faith, embracing John 16:13, which says, "the Spirit of truth will guide you into all truth." She entered a period of fervent prayer and meditation. Soon after, a meaningful dream provided distinct signs that directed her towards a specific role. Within weeks, this role not only matched her skill set but opened doors to opportunities and connections she hadn't anticipated. Samantha's experience showcases how attuning to the Holy Spirit can provide crucial insights during significant life changes.

Power in The Name of Jesus

Alicia faced a chronic health issue that had evolved into a significant mental and spiritual challenge. Determined to overcome, she held fast to the power contained in the name of Jesus, consistently declaring Philippians 2:10: "That at the name of Jesus every knee should bow." As she continued her daily faith-filled declarations, her symptoms began to improve significantly. Throughout her journey, Alicia experienced both empowerment and healing, which not only alleviated her condition but ignited a profound sense of gratitude and renewed purpose. Her transformation inspired those around her to lean into faith during their own hardships.

Transformation Through the Word of God

Struggling with a recent and profound loss, Tom was mired in despair and hopelessness. Before his turning point, he felt trapped in an endless cycle of grief and confusion. Upon rediscovering the Word of God, his path took a significant shift. Immersing himself in scriptures like Psalm 119:105, "Your word is a lamp for my feet, a light on my path," he unearthed guidance and renewed hope. By systematically memorizing and applying scripture to his daily life,

Tom transitioned from grief to a life of purpose, beginning to view obstacles as divinely aligned opportunities for growth.

These stories emphasize how personal faith, paired with divine principles, can lead to profound life changes even amidst dire circumstances.

Wrap-Up: Harnessing Spiritual Resources

These testimonies serve as powerful reminders of the spiritual resources available to believers. By wielding these divine tools, ordinary individuals can achieve extraordinary outcomes, transforming lives, opening doors, and renewing hope. Each narrative reinforces the lesson that faith, empowered by spiritual weapons, has the potential to break chains and create paths to victory. As believers harness these tools—through prayer, scripture, and the powerful invocation of divine guidance—they become examples of triumph, illuminating the way for others to follow. The profound changes experienced by Mary, John, Samantha, Alicia, and Tom demonstrate the lasting impact of consistency, faith, and spiritual resilience.

CHAPTER 16

NEVER LOSE A BATTLE AGAIN

Victory in spiritual warfare arises from consistently applying God's principles. To never lose a battle requires unwavering faith, discipline, and reliance on God's power.

- **Stay clothed in the full armor of God** (Ephesians 6:10-18).
- **Maintain unshakable faith** (Hebrews 10:23).
- **Engage in continuous prayer and fasting** (Matthew 17:21).
- **Walk in love and forgiveness** (Colossians 3:13).

Keys to Constant Victory:

1. Develop a lifestyle of prayer and worship (Luke 18:1).
2. Guard your heart and mind against negativity (Proverbs 4:23).

3. Speak life through daily declarations (Isaiah 57:19).

Occupy Till I Come

Jesus commands believers to "occupy till I come" (Luke 19:13), meaning we must actively advance God's kingdom while awaiting His return.

To occupy until Jesus returns means living with purpose every day, advancing His kingdom in all areas of life. The following examples illustrate how ordinary believers can embody this calling in practical, powerful ways.

- **Occupy through evangelism and discipleship** (Matthew 28:19-20).
- **Occupy through spiritual authority** (Luke 10:19).
- **Occupy through kingdom service** (Romans 12:11).

How to Occupy Effectively:

1. Use your gifts and callings for God's glory.
2. Engage in intercessory prayer for nations.
3. Take spiritual dominion in your sphere of influence.

Daily Life Examples of "Occupying Till Jesus Comes"

Example 1: Morning Routine with Purpose

John begins his day early, dedicating the first hour to reading the Bible and meditating on Scripture. This practice prepares his mind with positive, spiritually enriching content. After his devotion, he engages in prayer walks around his neighborhood, praying for local needs and seeking divine guidance on how he can serve throughout the day. As a result, John often experiences a deep sense of peace and spiritual alertness that empowers him to face challenges with purpose and clarity.

Example 2: Workplace Mission Field

Sarah works in an office where she views her responsibilities not just as job duties, but as opportunities for ministry. She fosters a spirit of encouragement within her team by consistently offering a listening ear and sharing positive, faith-based insights when appropriate. During breaks, she spends a few minutes in quiet reflection or writing in her prayer journal, subtly yet powerfully integrating her faith into her professional life. These practices cultivate a supportive atmosphere, leading to strengthened relationships and increased team morale.

Example 3: Community and Service

Each weekend, Alan volunteers at a local homeless shelter, using his gifts of administration and compassion to organize resources and spread love through his actions. He views this service as a direct extension of his faith, occupying his corner of the world with God's love. After serving, Alan gathers with other volunteers for a brief time of prayer and reflection, encouraging one another and sharing impactful testimonies. This practice has fostered a strong sense of community and mutual support among the volunteers, enhancing their collective commitment to serve.

Example 4: Family and Discipleship

Rachel prioritizes leading her family in daily devotions every evening. These sessions involve reading Bible stories, discussing their implications, and praying together. By engaging her children in active discussions about faith, she nurtures their spiritual growth and prepares them to become influencers in their own spheres as they mature. Through these practices, Rachel has observed improved family communication and a deeper understanding of faith among her children.

Example 5: Digital Evangelism

Mark leverages technology to share faith-inspired content on his social media platforms. He posts daily devotionals, inspirational quotes, and short video messages that challenge and encourage his followers to engage more deeply with their faith. Through these efforts, Mark reaches a wide audience, occupying digital spaces to expand God's kingdom. This initiative has resulted in a growing online community that fosters discussions and connections among like-minded individuals seeking spiritual growth.

By incorporating these examples into daily life, believers can continually advance God's kingdom and embody the command to "occupy till I come." Each act, no matter how small, contributes to a life lived in active expectation of His coming, fully engaging with spiritual authority and influence in various spheres.

Developing Daily Habits for Spiritual Power:

Daily Bread (Leviticus 6:12-13)

A victorious spiritual life requires discipline in seeking God daily. Leviticus 6:12-13 instructs priests to keep the fire on the altar burning, signifying the importance of consistency in spiritual devotion.

- **Daily prayer and Word study sustain spiritual fire** (Psalm 1:2).
- **Regular fasting renews spiritual strength** (Isaiah 40:31).
- **Practicing gratitude aligns you with divine blessings** (Philippians 4:6-7).

Steps to Mastering Daily Disciplines:

1. Set aside time for personal devotion each day.
2. Meditate on scripture and apply it.
3. Maintain a spirit of worship throughout the day.

4. By implementing these principles, believers can experience consistent victory, fulfill their divine purpose, and walk in God's power.

Highly Recommended Disciplines

To truly walk in spiritual victory, it's not enough to know the principles; you must also practice them with disciplined consistency. Just as in any army, training is essential before deployment, and the same holds true in spiritual warfare.

You will undergo training, and upon completion, you will receive your uniform, equipment, tools of service, and your identity card.

Your training will be ongoing as long as you are in service. The same requirements apply when you become a born-again child of God. Here are a few disciplines you will need to practice daily or weekly if you want to lead a victorious Christian life, be strong in the Lord, and recover everything you have ever lost.

Regular Disciplines:

These disciplines are not mandatory like they would be in the military or police department, which explains why many believers do not enjoy the full benefits of salvation. You must choose to be different and lead yourself from victory to victory. Run to obtain the prize, strive for mastery, and exercise self-control in all things; bring your body under subjection

(1 Corinthians 9:24-27). Here are a few disciplines you should make a habit:

1. Read or listen to your Bible every day for at least one hour.

2. Practice speaking the Word for at least 10 minutes daily; faith comes by hearing (Romans 10:17). Alternatively, you can use the 50/10 power formula: read the same material, section, or chapters of the Bible for 50 minutes, then review that area and read it aloud for 10 minutes each day. Practice reading the same material for 30 days at a time. This approach will help you better understand and apply what you are studying. Aim for mastery, not just bragging rights that you read your Bible (1 Corinthians 9:25).

3. Put on your God-designed and given uniform daily. Just as police officers and military personnel have uniforms that identify them and allow them to command authority, we as believers are also instructed to don our uniform each day, as stated in Ephesians 6:10-19. This is the whole armor of God, and we are commanded to put it on without ever being told to take it off. You must always be ready.

4. Give generously and consistently of your resources, at least as often as you receive an income (Matthew 6:3-4).

5. Pray regularly (Matthew 6:5-7). In Matthew 26:40-44, Jesus asked his disciples to pray for at least an hour.

6. Fast regularly (Matthew 6:17-18). In Luke 18:12-14, the Pharisee mentioned that he fasted twice a week.

7. Find a local church where you can fellowship and serve regularly, ideally for at least 1 to 2 days a week (Hebrews 10:24-26, Psalm 84:7, Acts 2:46-47).

Develop Your Faith in Constant and Never-Ending Weapons Training

Make up your mind to continue developing your strength and faith. Be focused, determined, resilient, and persistent. Get planted in the house of God so you can flourish. It is those who are planted and wholeheartedly attend to the things of God—like Joshua and Caleb—who reach the land of promise (Deuteronomy 1:36-38).

Those who dwell—not just visit—the secret place of the Most High enjoy constant divine protection (Psalm 91:1). When you make His presence your permanent home rather than an occasional stop, you gain access to unmatched strength and safety. Like Joshua and Caleb, stay rooted in God's house and fully engaged in His work to reach your promised land (Deuteronomy 1:36–38).

Appear in Zion regularly. It is those who appear in Zion who go from strength to strength, and that is what this guide is all about (Psalm 84:7). Developing strength, faith, and capacity enables you to overcome the issues of life on command.

Finally, remember these words of Jesus and meditate on them regularly: "No one who puts a hand to the plow and looks back is fit for service in the kingdom of God" (Luke 9:62). You are worthy of the kingdom, brother, sister, father, mother, and whoever you are.

By implementing these principles, believers can live in consistent victory, fulfilling their divine purpose and walking in God's power.

Grace and blessings to you (Numbers 6:22-26).

Sample Weekly Schedule for Daily Spiritual Disciplines

The following weekly routine serves as a model to help you build consistency in your spiritual disciplines. You can adjust the times and activities based on your personal schedule, but the goal is to keep your spiritual fire burning daily.

Monday:

- **Morning:**
    - **Devotion (30 minutes):** Start your day with meditation on Ephesians 6:10-18, focusing on putting on the full armor of God.

- - **Prayer (15 minutes):** Pray for guidance and strength for the week; include prayers for others in your community.
- **Afternoon:**
  - **Bible Study (30 minutes):** Study a chapter of Proverbs to gain wisdom and insight.
- **Evening:**
  - **Reflection (15 minutes):** Reflect on your day's challenges and victories, expressing gratitude.

Tuesday:

- **Morning:**
  - **Worship (15 minutes):** Engage in uplifting spiritual songs that motivate you.
  - **Scripture Reading (30 minutes):** Continue Bible reading with the Gospels, focusing on Jesus' teachings.
- **Afternoon:**
  - **Journaling (15 minutes):** Write down insights gathered from the scripture and how they apply to your day.
- **Evening:**
  - **Intercessory Prayer (20 minutes):** Pray for world events and individuals in need.

Wednesday:

- **Morning:**
    - **Meditation (30 minutes):** Focus on forgiveness (Colossians 3:13) and release any personal grievances.
- **Afternoon:**
    - **Community Service Planning (30 minutes):** Plan an act of kindness or community service for the weekend.
- **Evening:**
    - **Bible Group (1 Hour):** Participate in a virtual or in-person Bible study group.

Thursday:

- **Morning:**
    - **Fasting & Prayer (Skip breakfast):** Combine fasting with prayers focused on spiritual growth and strength.
- **Afternoon:**
    - **Scripture Declaration (15 minutes):** Speak declarations of God's promises over your life.
- **Evening:**
    - **Reflection (15 minutes):** Evaluate how fasting has affected your spiritual awareness.

Friday:

- **Morning:**
  - **Prayer Walk (30 minutes):** Go for a walk, praying and worshiping as you enjoy God's creation.
- **Afternoon:**
  - **Study (30 minutes):** Focus on the principles of spiritual warfare from Ephesians.
- **Evening:**
  - **Family Prayer Time (30 minutes):** Pray together as a family, sharing insights and prayer requests.

Saturday:

- **Morning:**
  - **Extended Devotion (1 Hour):** Take time to delve deeper into scripture or a spiritual book.
- **Afternoon:**
  - **Volunteer Activity (2 Hours):** Engage in an activity that serves your local community.
- **Evening:**
  - **Gratitude Journaling (15 minutes):** Note down the blessings you are thankful for throughout the week.

Sunday:

- **Morning:**
    - **Church Service (4 Hours):** Attend a local church service and actively engage with the community.
- **Afternoon:**
    - **Replenish Quiet Time (1 Hour):** Reflect on the sermon and consider its application to your life.
- **Evening:**
    - **Family Bible Study (1 Hour):** Host a relaxed Bible reading and discussion session with your family.

This schedule serves as an example designed to instill strong spiritual practices and resilience, ensuring readiness for spiritual warfare while fostering personal and communal growth. Adjust timings and activities according to your personal needs and commitments.

Action Plan Recap

1. **Maintain Spiritual Preparedness:** Equip yourself daily with the full armor of God, embracing spiritual disciplines such as regular prayer and fasting. This preparation not only readies you for battles but also aligns you with God's strength and resilience (Ephesians 6:10-18).

2. **Cultivate a Prayerful Lifestyle:** Develop consistency in prayer and worship. Set aside specific times each day for personal devotion, allowing these moments to fuel your spiritual fire and fortify your heart against negativity and doubt (Matthew 17:21).

3. **Exercise Love and Forgiveness:** Walk in love and resolve any unforgiveness. Love shields you spiritually and keeps your heart clean and open to God's guidance and blessings (Colossians 3:13).

4. **Occupy Through Active Engagement:** Utilize your gifts and spiritual authority for God's kingdom. Engage in activities like evangelism, discipleship, and community service, empowering you to effectively hold spiritual ground (Luke 19:13; Matthew 28:19-20).

5. **Master Daily Disciplines:** Commit to daily scriptural study, consistent generosity, and maintaining gratitude. These practices will align your life with divine blessings and ensure ongoing spiritual growth and victory (Philippians 4:6-7; Leviticus 6:11-12).

By regularly practicing these disciplines, you are better positioned to achieve constant victory in spiritual warfare and live fulfilled in your divine purpose.

ACKNOWLEDGEMENT

First and foremost we want to acknowledge and give thanks to our Heavenly Father, the Lord Jesus Christ and the Holy Spirit for the opportunity to be a part of the Kingdom of God. Next we want to acknowledge everyone who has played one role or another in our lives, whether in person, through books, audios, videos, conferences etc. Special thanks to our family members and relatives worldwide. Our senior Pastor at Overcomers Christian Fellowship where we fellowship, Pastor Benny Momoh for his support and encouragement over the years, the whole Church membership and also to the faithful members of our Tuesday Night Bible study and Prayer Meeting. Finally we want to say a big thank you to our Sister Ramoma O., who encouraged us to re-start our Tuesday Night Bible Study after Covid-19 temporarily shut us down.

To everyone who will ever read this book or listen to the audio: Thank you. We wish you meaning and a transformed life as you apply the message in it.

ABOUT THE AUTHORS

AUTHORS OF SUCCESS: IT'S YOUR BIRTHRIGHT

Larry and Denise Adebesin are self-help authors dedicated to empowering individuals through transformative, Christ-centered principles. Since publishing their first book in 1996, they have authored five influential works focused on inspiring and transforming lives with proven biblical insights. Larry and Denise's writing career is distinguished by their commitment to personal and spiritual growth. Their books, recognized for their impact, have been a testament to their passion for enriching lives through Christ centered and biblically based literature. Larry's extensive background as a Licensed Life Insurance since 1990, specializing in Infinite Banking and Wealth Accumulation Life Insurance Policies (WALI's) adds depth to their empowering messages. The couple, married since 1993, and also serve as Associate Pastors at Overcomers

Christian Fellowship in Lithonia, Georgia, embodying their teachings in everyday life, under the leadership of Pastor Benny Momoh. As lifelong learners, Larry and Denise continue to explore new avenues to inspire their audience, with exciting projects on the horizon to further extend their influence and support.

www.ingramcontent.com/pod-product-compliance
Lightning Source LLC
Chambersburg PA
CBHW032046150426
43194CB00006B/443